Chocolate!

GALLERY BOOKS
An Imprint of W. H. Smith Publishers Inc.
112 Madison Avenue
New York City 10016

Editor Patricia Hitchcock
Art editor Steve Wilson
Production Richard Churchill

U.S. Consultant Annie Lurie

Published by
GALLERY BOOKS
An imprint of W.H.Smith Publishers Inc.
112 Madison Avenue, New York,
New York 10016

Typeset in Melior Roman
by Litho Link Limited, Welshpool

Printed and bound in Hong Kong by
Dai Nippon Printing Company

ISBN 0 8317 1289-9

Contents

ALL ABOUT CHOCOLATE

Ever since chocolate was first introduced to Europe from Mexico, after its discovery by Spaniards in the early sixteenth century, it has been highly regarded as one of the most luxurious of sweetmeats and flavorings. It was made into a popular beverage in the coffee and chocolate houses of Dr. Johnson's London, and in the contemporary French court. Bars of chocolate were not made for nearly 200 years: the secret of expressing the cocoa butter from the beans was finally discovered in the eighteenth century by a Dutchman, Van Houten.

As well as its endless uses in sweet dishes, chocolate is used in various countries as a savory flavoring, usually with game or poultry. The amount of chocolate used in such dishes is small but it enriches the sauce and lends it a smooth texture and subtle flavor.

Chocolate and cocoa are both made from the beans of the cacao tree (*Theobroma cacao*), which grows in Africa and South America. The word "cocoa" is the English corruption of cacao, while the word "chocolate" comes from the Mexican drink *chocolatl*, a thin and bitter brew considered to be an aphrodisiac. In Mexico, the beans were highly prized and even used in some areas as a currency.

After gathering, the beans are fermented, roasted and crushed to produce a thick liquid containing about 50% fat, called cocoa butter.

Cocoa is made by extracting half the cocoa butter from the liquid, leaving a solid block that is then ground into a powder. To make chocolate, extra cocoa butter is added to the liquid, together with varying amounts of sugar. The mixture is then refined and molded.

Chocolate is rich in iron and calcium and also contains protein, fat and carbohydrate. There are three main groups of chocolate, plus two common powdered forms:

Dessert Chocolate
For eating bars or filled candies, a particularly refined chocolate with a high proportion of cocoa butter is used. Chocolate bars can be used for cooking but are less suitable than cooking chocolate.

Dark chocolate – sometimes labelled "bitter" – is widely used in cooking, as well as being popular as a dessert chocolate. Bitter chocolate has less sugar than dark chocolate and also has a stronger chocolate flavor.

Milk chocolate, as its name suggests, has milk added and is milder and blander than dark chocolate. It can separate when heated, and so is not normally used for cooking. It can be grated as a decoration, or carefully melted for spreading onto cookies or cakes.

Baking Chocolate
Baking chocolate is a semi-sweet, usually dark chocolate and is excellent for use in baking. It must contain at least 34% cocoa solids (the legal minimum for any product labeled "chocolate"). In the United States, unsweetened chocolate may be used instead of semi-sweet if the sugar is increased by 4 teaspoons per 1 oz of chocolate. Baking chocolate tends to be softer than dessert chocolate because it has a higher fat content to make it melt more readily; it does not grate easily. If it is difficult to obtain locally, use dark chocolate instead (see above).

Confectioner's Chocolate
Confectioner's chocolate, also known as *couverture*, is of high quality and is ideal for cake decorating or for icing cakes, as it gives a smooth, shiny finish.

Cocoa Powder and Chocolate for drinks
Cocoa powder is unsweetened and contains less cocoa butter than chocolate. It is a starchy substance and needs to be cooked. It is used primarily for baking and drinks. Drinking chocolate is pre-cooked cocoa with added sugar and flavorings. It blends easily with hot or cold liquids but is not intended for cooking.

CHOCOLATE SUBSTITUTES

Prepared Frosting
Milk and dark covering – sometimes flavored with oranges or peppermint – cost less than real chocolate and cannot be labeled as chocolate. Chocolate substitutes are normally labeled as chocolate-flavored.

Carob
Although many people find the taste of carob similar to that of chocolate, it contains none of the substances that cause allergies to chocolate. Carob powder is the ground pod of a Mediterranean fruit and is widely available in health food shops. It can be used in place of cocoa powder. It is naturally sweet, so reduce the sugar by about a quarter.

Emergency Chocolate
Blend 6 tablespoons cocoa powder with 2 tablespoons vegetable oil and 3-4 tablespoons sugar for every 2 oz chocolate.

STORING CHOCOLATE

Cocoa and chocolate should be stored in a cool, dry place. Cocoa will keep for about 1 year in a tightly sealed tin. Chocolate will keep for about 6 months. Chocolate stored at too high a temperature or in a refrigerator will develop a misty, white bloom, caused by the fat rising to the surface. This will not affect its flavor. Always keep chocolate well wrapped, as it will absorb the flavors of other foods.

MELTING CHOCOLATE

When using chocolate in cooking, it is often necessary to melt it first. The best method of doing this is to break the chocolate into pieces and to put these in a bowl over a saucepan half full of simmering water or in a double boiler. Keep the water at simmering point to prevent steam rising, as this will make the chocolate cloudy and granular and too stiff to work.

As soon as the chocolate begins to soften, remove the pan from the heat and stir gently until all the pieces have melted. It is best not to stir until the chocolate has almost melted, as it can become granular. Always allow to cool slightly before adding to puddings, cakes or desserts.

Never heat chocolate in a pan over direct heat, as it scorches easily and the resultant bitter flavor is impossible to mask or to eliminate.

To melt chocolate in a microwave oven, put the pieces in a glass bowl and microwave at 30% (low) for 1-2 minutes, watching carefully.

DECORATING WITH CHOCOLATE

Chocolate can be used in many ways to add a finishing touch to cakes or desserts.

Grated Chocolate

Use the coarse section of a sharp grater. It is worth using an electric grater only if you are making a large quantity of grated chocolate. Use for sprinkling over cakes, trifles, soufflés or desserts, or for coating the sides of cakes. Always chill the chocolate for at least 20 minutes before using it. This helps to stop it melting quickly in the warmth of your hand.

Chocolate Curls

Use a sharp vegetable peeler to scrape curls from the flat, unridged side of a bar or block, working downwards. Bring the chocolate to room temperature for really long, thin curls. Beware of melting the block with your fingers. If it starts to melt, replace in the refrigerator to chill a little.

Chocolate Caraque

Caraque is really a long chocolate curl, but looks much more sophisticated on some dishes. Melt dark chocolate (see page 9) and pour it onto an oiled cookie sheet or other cold, flat surface (marble is best). Spread it out evenly with a palette knife. Leave until completely cold and set. Using a long-bladed, sharp knife, shave away from you with a light pressure, angling the blade at about 45° to the surface. Use wooden toothpicks to transfer these delicate rolls to the top of a cake or dessert.

Chocolate Shapes

Melt dark chocolate (see page 9). Trace small designs such as stars, flowers or numerals on waxed paper and outline or fill in the shapes by piping the melted chocolate through a very fine icing nozzle. Melted chocolate sets quite quickly, so make a few small waxed paper piping bags and use only a little chocolate at a time, keeping the rest over simmering water.

When the chocolate has set, peel away the paper very carefully. Alternatively, pipe the shapes directly onto a cake or dessert. To make shell or star borders, thicken the chocolate slightly with 1 or 2 drops of glycerine, so that it will hold its shape. Stir until the chocolate thickens, then spoon carefully into a piping bag with a suitable nozzle and pipe the border in the normal way.

For solid chocolate shapes, cut cardboard stencils and lay them on top of a thin layer of melted chocolate, spread on waxed paper and allowed to cool. Then cut around the stencils with a knife. Cookie cutters can be used to cut out simpler shapes.

Chocolate Rose Leaves

There are two methods for making rose leaves, which make an enchanting decoration for cakes and ice-creams. Either melt chocolate (see page 9), spread it thinly on waxed paper and leave to set before cutting out leaf shapes and marking the veins

Decorating with chocolate

1 Chocolate curls: scraping from a bar with a peeler.
2 Chocolate caraque: shaving from set chocolate with a sharp knife.
3 Piped shapes: piping onto waxed paper.
4 Solid shapes: using a cutter.
5 and 6 Chocolate rose leaves: coating in chocolate, then peeling away the rose leaves.

with a fork or, for a more professional finish, use real rose leaves as a "mold".

Melt chocolate (see page 9). Wash and dry the leaves gently. Using fingers or tweezers, press the leaves one at a time, shiny side up, on to the melted chocolate. The underside of the leaf should be coated. Carefully move the leaf to the side of the plate and draw it across the edge to remove excess chocolate. (Alternatively, use an artist's paintbrush to coat the leaves.)

Place the leaves, chocolate side up, on waxed paper and allow to set in a cool place. Do not chill, as this will cause the chocolate to "bloom". Once the chocolate has set, carefully peel away the leaves.

Chocolate Cases

To make attractive and tasty containers for whipped cream, fruit or small pieces of iced cake, use tartlet molds. Foil or paper cupcake liners or sweet cases also work well. Brush each lightly with flavorless vegetable oil and set aside, inverted, to drain. Melt chocolate (see page 9), allow to cool slightly, then carefully spoon into the molds so that the chocolate lines the bottom. Pick the mold up and spoon in more chocolate, rotating the mold as you do so, to coat the sides thinly. Chill until the chocolate is set.

Turn the mold upside-down; tap gently to release the chocolate cases and chill again to firm before filling.

Chocolate Sprinkles

These are tiny, fine strands of chocolate or chocolate-flavored sugar, ideal for sprinkling over cakes or desserts or for coating the sides or top of cakes decoratively.

Cocoa Powder

As well as making a useful swift topping for drinks, sweetened cocoa powder can be used for dredging over cakes or desserts, for a sweeter flavor. This is most effective if contrasted with powdered sugar. Dredge with powdered sugar, then arrange strips of foil or waxed paper to make a symmetrical pattern. Sieve the chocolate or cocoa powder over the top of the cake or dessert, then carefully remove the foil.

ICINGS AND FILLINGS

Icing is a tasty and attractive way of finishing most cakes, and chocolate is ideally suited to every kind from shiny glacé to soft, creamy butter frosting.

Glacé Icing
Glacé icing is the simplest of all the icings.

Chocolate glacé icing has a richness and density that makes it ideal for covering cakes with a smooth, shiny coating that needs no further decoration. You can also use it for piping fine designs and writing, and for simple designs such as "feathering" (see right).

Butter Cream
Butter creams are soft creamy frostings, which are used as fillings as well as toppings. They are easy to spread and swirl and are frequently used around the side of a cake to hold chopped nuts or chocolate sprinklings.

They are made by creaming butter and sugar together until light and fluffy. Flavoring and coloring are then added. For extra richness, egg yolks may be added, too.

French butter cream, known as crème au beurre, is made from the same ingredients but they are combined in a more elaborate way. The sugar is boiled with water to make a syrup. This is then poured onto the yolks, whisking to make a fluffy sauce. Butter is then creamed in for extra smoothness.

Both these butter creams are used in the same way. Smooth on the frosting fairly thickly and use a fork or palette knife to decorate the cake. These frostings also pipe well.

Fudge Icings and Frostings
Icings made from melted ingredients are ideal fillings as well as toppings. The simplest are made from melted chocolate with butter or cream stirred in. Or, you can make fudge by boiling together the sugar and cream and then beating in the butter.

Icing A Cake
To keep a cake plate clean and free from icing trails, cut 4 strips of waxed paper or foil. Lay the strips in a square pattern around the rim of the plate and place the cake carefully on the strips, making sure the cake rests on the paper all around. When you have finished icing, carefully remove the strips from under the cake.

Feathering Glacé Icing
Feathering is usually done as a dark design on a white background, but the opposite of a pale feather on chocolate icing is just as effective. Ice the cake with chocolate glacé icing. While this is still soft, pipe parallel lines about ¾ inch apart in a contrasting color across the cake. Quickly draw a skewer at right angles across the piping, at the same intervals, drawing it alternately in opposite directions to give a feathered effect. Wipe the skewer each time.

Cobweb Decoration
Cover a cake in chocolate icing, then pipe a contrasting color in a spiral on the top of the cake. Draw a skewer alternately into and out from the center, to give a cobweb effect.

Swirled Frosting
Work outwards from the center with a palette knife for a smooth effect (see picture).

EASY CHOCOLATE FROSTING

(makes about 1 cup)
7 oz dark chocolate, broken into pieces
½ cup sour cream
⅛ teaspoon salt

1 Melt the broken chocolate (see page 9).
2 Remove from the heat and stir in the sour cream and salt. Spread over the cake at once.

GLACE ICING

(covers an 8½ in cake)
¾ cup confectioner's sugar
2 tablespoons unsweetened cocoa powder, sifted
3 tablespoons apricot jam

1 Sift the confectioner's sugar and cocoa into the top of a double boiler.
2 Add 3 tablespoons plus 1 teaspoon water. Stir with a wooden spoon over a low heat. Do not let the water in the bottom of the double boiler get too hot, or the icing will be lumpy.
3 The icing is the right consistency when it coats the back of a spoon. If necessary, stiffen it by adding a little extra confectioner's sugar.
4 Place the cake to be iced on a wire rack over a cookie sheet or waxed paper. Strain the jam into a small saucepan, add 1 tablespoon water and heat gently. When the jam has completely melted, let it stand a moment or two and then brush the warm glaze over the cake.
5 While the glacé icing is still soft, pour it over the cake and guide it down the sides with a palette knife to cover them completely.

BUTTER CREAM

(fills and covers a 8½ in 2 layer cake)
1 stick butter, softened
1 cup confectioner's sugar, sifted
4 oz unsweetened chocolate, melted and slightly cooled, or 4 tablespoons unsweetened cocoa powder

[1] Beat the butter with a wooden spoon or an electric mixer until light and fluffy.
[2] Gradually beat in the confectioner's sugar, a few spoonfuls at a time.
[3] Add the chocolate or cocoa and mix well.
[4] If you wish to make butter cream in advance, keep it in the refrigerator and bring it out to soften before use.

CREME AU BEURRE

(fills and covers a 8½ in 2 layer cake)
3 large egg yolks
⅓ cup granulated sugar
1½ sticks sweet butter, softened
4 oz dark chocolate, melted and slightly cooled, or 4 tablespoons cocoa powder

[1] Lightly beat the egg yolks in a bowl.
[2] In a small pan, heat the sugar with ¼ cup water until dissolved. Bring it to a boil and boil for a few minutes until the temperature on a sugar thermometer reaches 115C /240F. At this temperature, a sample dropped into cold water will form a soft ball between your fingers. The syrup must not be allowed to heat above this temperature, so start testing it early on.
[3] As soon as the syrup is ready, immediately pour it onto the egg yolks all at once as you beat them – this is easiest with an electric beater. Continue beating until the mixture is pale, cool, very thick and mousse-like.
[4] In another bowl, cream the butter until it is really soft and the same consistency as the egg yolk mixture. Gradually beat the creamed butter into the egg yolk mixture, a tiny bit at a time to begin with until the mixture thickens, when it can be added more quickly. When all the butter is beaten in, add the chocolate or cocoa.

CHOCOLATE RUM ICING

(covers the top of a 8½ in cake)
2 oz semi-sweet chocolate
2 tablespoons butter
1 tablespoon rum

[1] Break the chocolate into pieces and melt it in the top of a double boiler or a bowl over simmering water. Beat in the butter. Add the rum and continue to beat until the icing is glossy. Leave to cool and harden a little.

[2] Pour the icing over the top of the cake, spread evenly with a palette knife and allow to set.

SAUCES

Chocolate sauce makes the simplest dessert special. Here are three useful versions.

QUICK CHOCOLATE SAUCE

4 oz semi-sweet chocolate
2 tablespoons sweet butter

[1] Melt the chocolate and butter in a bowl over simmering water with 4 tablespoons water.

For a more exotic flavor: replace 2 tablespoons of the water with brandy or rum.

CHOCOLATE VANILLA SAUCE

2 oz semi-sweet chocolate
½ cup milk
sugar to taste
2 drops vanilla extract

[1] Melt the chocolate in the milk, stirring constantly. Add sugar and vanilla while stirring.
[2] When the sugar is dissolved and the chocolate melted, remove from the heat. Serve hot or cold.

CHOCOLATE-ALMOND SAUCE

6 oz semi-sweet chocolate, broken into pieces
1¾ cups condensed milk
1 teaspoon vanilla extract
¼ teaspoon almond extract

[1] Melt the chocolate with the milk, stirring occasionally.
[2] As soon as the chocolate melts, remove from the heat and beat in the extracts.
[3] Continue beating until the sauce is smooth. Serve warm.

DRINKS

Chocolate Liqueurs
These are produced by either macerating or percolating cocoa beans, then distilling and sweetening. The usual name for chocolate liqueur is Crème de Cacao. Liqueurs are excellent for use in mousses and frozen desserts, hot sauces and soufflés. They can also be poured over ice cream or folded into whipped cream.

HOT CHOCOLATE MILK

(makes 1 cup)
1½ oz semi-sweet chocolate
1 cup boiling milk

[1] Melt the chocolate with just enough milk to moisten it, then stir in the remaining, boiling milk until evenly blended.
[2] Beat until frothy and serve piping hot, sprinkled with ground cinnamon or nutmeg.

VARIATIONS
Add an egg yolk and top with cream for Viennese Chocolate. Add 6 tablespoons strong black coffee for Mocha Chocolate; top with marshmallows.

CHOCOLATE RUM PUNCH

(serves 10)
¾ cup granulated sugar
¼ cup cocoa powder
2 cups milk
1 cup dark rum
1 cup light cream
½ cup orange-flavored liqueur
ice cubes, to serve

[1] Mix the sugar and cocoa together and warm over a low heat, gradually stirring in the milk until the mixture is smooth. Simmer, stirring, for 1 minute. Allow to cool.

[2] Stir in the rum, cream and liqueur. Chill. Serve over ice in punch cups or tumblers.

THE COOKIE JAR

Cookies, picnic bars and brownies are quick and easy to make and always popular, and here's a range of recipes to suit every taste. Serve delicate Chocolate Kisses for elegant tea parties or take along chocolatey Rocky Road Brownies for a great children's picnic. Many bars and cookies store well, too – so why not make a batch and keep them for unexpected visitors?

NUTTY CHOCOLATE TRIANGLES

Preparation time: 15 minutes
Baking time: 30–35 minutes
Cooling time: 30 minutes
Finishing time: 10 minutes
Makes 8

vegetable oil, for greasing
¾ cup all-purpose flour
2 tablespoons cocoa powder
½ teaspoon baking powder
pinch of salt
6 tablespoons margarine
⅓ cup light soft brown sugar firmly packed
⅓ cup light corn syrup
¼ teaspoon vanilla extract
2 eggs
3 tablespoons hazelnut chocolate spread
chopped, roasted hazelnuts, to finish

1 Preheat the oven to 350F. Grease a 7 inch square pan, about 1 inch deep. Line the base with waxed paper, then lightly grease the paper.

2 Sift the flour, cocoa, baking powder and salt into a bowl and reserve.

3 Beat the margarine, sugar and syrup until pale and fluffy, then beat in the vanilla. Beat in the eggs, one at a time, adding 1 tablespoon flour mixture with each egg. Stir in the remaining flour mixture with a wooden spoon, then beat briefly until smooth and evenly blended.

4 Pour the mixture into the prepared pan, level the surface, then make a hollow in the center. Bake in the oven for 30–35 minutes, or until springy to the touch. (Cover with waxed paper towards the end of baking to avoid overbrowning.)

5 Cool the cake for 5 minutes, then run a palette knife around the sides, turn out onto a wire rack and peel off the lining paper. Lay a clean dish towel over the wire rack to prevent the mesh marking the soft cake. Turn the cake right way up and leave it to cool completely.

6 To finish: Trim off the crusty edges, then cover the top with hazelnut spread. Cut the cake into 4 squares then cut each square in half diagonally to make 8 triangles. Decorate with chopped, roasted hazelnuts.

7 The cold (unfinished) cake can be wrapped in plastic wrap and stored in an airtight container for 4 days.

CHEWY BARS

Preparation time: 10 minutes
Baking time: 30–35 minutes
Cooling time: 30 minutes
Finishing time: 10 minutes
Makes 16

margarine, for greasing
2 sticks margarine or butter
1 scant cup quick-cooking oats
¼ cup flaked almonds
½ cup soft brown sugar firmly packed
¾ cup shredded coconut
4 oz semi-sweet chocolate, broken into pieces
2 tablespoons flaked almonds, to finish

1 Preheat the oven to 300F. Grease a 12 × 8 inch baking pan.

2 Put the margarine or butter into a large, heavy-based pan and melt gently over very low heat, stirring occasionally. Remove from the heat, add the oats, almonds, sugar and coconut and mix together thoroughly.

3 Spoon the mixture into the prepared pan and press evenly over the base of the pan using the back of a dampened, large metal spoon.

4 Bake in the oven for 30–35 minutes, until set and golden brown. Cool for 5 minutes, then cut into 16 bars. Leave in the pan to cool completely.

5 Melt the chocolate pieces (see page 9).

6 Meanwhile, transfer the bars to a wire rack and place a plate underneath.

7 Remove the bowl with the chocolate from above the simmering water and spread the melted chocolate over the top of each bar. Sprinkle with flaked almonds while the chocolate is still soft and leave to set completely.

8 The bars can be stored in an airtight tin for up to 4 days.

CHOCOLATE KISSES

Preparation time: 30 minutes
Baking time: 15 minutes
Cooling time: 30 minutes
Makes 15

vegetable oil, for greasing
¾ cup margarine or butter, softened
bare ½ cup confectioner's sugar
1½ cups all-purpose flour
2 tablespoons cocoa powder
confectioner's sugar, to finish

ORANGE FILLING
¼ cup margarine or butter, softened
¾ cup confectioner's sugar
grated rind of 1 orange
1 teaspoon orange juice

1. Preheat the oven to 375F. Grease a large cookie sheet with vegetable oil.

2. Beat the margarine or butter and confectioner's sugar together until pale and fluffy.

3. Sift the flour and cocoa powder into a separate bowl. Using an electric beater or a wooden spoon, gradually work the flour mixture into the fluffy sugar mixture to make a soft, sticky dough.

4. Put the dough into a piping bag fitted with a large star nozzle and pipe about 30 small rosettes on to the cookie sheet. For each rosette, hold the bag upright and close to the surface of the cookie sheet. Exerting gentle pressure, move the nozzle in a tight, complete circle. Lift nozzle sharply.

5. Bake the cookies in the oven for 15 minutes, or until firm underneath. Check that the undersides of the cookies are firm and set before removing them from the oven, otherwise they will crumble.

6. Cool the cookies on the cookie sheet for 5 minutes, then use a palette knife or spatula to transfer them to a wire rack. Leave to cool completely.

7. Meanwhile, make the filling: beat the margarine and confectioner's sugar together until pale and fluffy, then beat in the orange rind and juice.

8. Sandwich the kisses together in pairs with the filling. Sift confectioner's sugar lightly over the top and serve within 1–2 hours.

9. The unfilled cookies can be stored in an airtight container for 1 week. Once filled, they should be eaten the same day.

VARIATIONS
For hazelnut kisses, place a skinned hazelnut in the center of each rosette before baking.

Illustrated on page 15.

ALMOND COOKIES

Preparation time: 20 minutes
Baking time: 1–1¼ hours
Cooling time: 30 minutes
Finishing time: 35–45 minutes
Makes 10

2 large egg whites
½ cup granulated sugar
¾ cup ground almonds
2 oz dark chocolate, melted, to finish (see page 9)

CHOCOLATE BUTTER CREAM
bare ½ cup confectioner's sugar
2 teaspoons cocoa powder
2 tablespoons butter, softened

1 Preheat the oven to 275F. Line 2 cookie sheets with non-stick vegetable parchment paper or oiled waxed paper.

2 In a clean, dry bowl, beat the egg whites until standing in stiff peaks. Beat in the sugar, 1 tablespoon at a time, until the meringue is stiff and glossy. Fold in the ground almonds.

3 Put the mixture into a piping bag fitted with a large plain nozzle. Pipe twenty 2 inch rounds onto cookie sheets, about 1 inch apart.

4 Bake below center of oven for 1–1¼ hours, until firm and crisp. Swap sheets halfway through baking. Peel the paper off the rounds while warm, then cool completely.

5 Make the buttercream: sift confectioner's sugar with cocoa. Beat the butter until very soft, then slowly beat in the sugar mixture and 1 teaspoon hot water.

6 Sandwich the rounds in pairs with buttercream, then refrigerate for 15–20 minutes.

7 To finish, hold each cookie on its side and dip into the melted chocolate so that one edge is well coated. Leave on a wire rack to set.

8 The cookies will keep fresh for 1–2 days in an airtight container in a cool place. Do not store in the refrigerator as the cookies will lose their crispness.

HONEY NUT BROWNIES

Preparation time: 10 minutes
Baking time: 25–35 minutes
Cooling time: 30 minutes
Makes 16

- vegetable oil, for greasing
- 2 oz semi-sweet chocolate, broken into pieces
- 1 stick butter
- ½ cup clear honey
- 2 eggs
- 1 teaspoon vanilla extract
- 1½ cups all-purpose flour
- ¾ teaspoon baking powder
- ½ teaspoon salt
- 3 tablespoons cocoa powder
- ½ cup chopped walnuts

[1] Preheat the oven to 325F. Grease a 7 inch square cake pan.

[2] Put the chocolate pieces and butter in a bowl over a pan of just simmering water. Do not stir until the chocolate has melted and the pan is removed from the heat.

[3] Put the honey, eggs and vanilla in a bowl and add the melted chocolate mixture. Beat together with a fork until smooth.

[4] Sift the flour, baking powder, salt and cocoa powder into the bowl and beat together with the chocolate and egg mixture. Stir in the walnuts.

[5] Pour the mixture into the prepared pan and spread it out evenly, using the dampened back of a metal spoon.

[6] Bake for 25–35 minutes or until a skewer inserted into the center of the brownies comes out clean.

[7] Cool in the pan, then cut into 16 squares, using a sharp knife.

[8] Serve topped with whipped cream, or with ice cream for a special dessert.

[9] Brownies keep well for a day or two. Keep covered in an airtight tin or wrapped in aluminium foil.

ROCKY ROAD BROWNIES

Preparation time: 10 minutes
Baking time: 30 minutes
Finishing time: 15 minutes
Cooling time: 30–40 minutes
Makes 12

- 1 lb package brownie mix
- 2 eggs
- 3 cups miniature marshmallows
- ¾ cup chopped salted peanuts
- 1 oz unsweetened baking chocolate
- 2 tablespoons butter or margarine
- ½ teaspoon vanilla extract
- 1 cup confectioner's sugar, sifted

[1] Prepare the brownie mix according to the directions on the package for making cake-type brownies, adding the 2 eggs called for in the package directions.

[2] As soon as the brownies have been removed from the oven, scatter the marshmallows and chopped peanuts over the top; press them down lightly with your fingertips. Cool in the pan on the wire rack.

[3] Melt the chocolate and butter in a heavy saucepan over a low heat. Remove from the heat; stir in the vanilla, the icing sugar and 1 tablespoon boiling water until the mixture is smooth. (Add a little more boiling water if the mixture seems too thick.) Drizzle the melted chocolate over the marshmallows and peanuts in a zig-zag pattern.

[4] Allow the decorated brownies to stand for at least 30 minutes, until the chocolate is set. Cut into squares and loosen the cake around the sides of the pan. Serve the brownies directly from the pan.

[5] Store in the pan, covered in foil. The brownies will keep well for 2–3 days.

PASTRIES AND PIES

All over the world, people love the combination of chocolate and pastry: Chocolate Pie is as American as the Statue of Liberty, and European variations include feathery French Brioches and Eclairs and delicious Chocolate Bakewell from England. And for a special dinner, what could be more dramatic than a pyramid of profiteroles, coated with rich chocolate sauce?

AMERICAN CHOCOLATE PIE

Preparation time: 1 hour
Setting time: 30 minutes
Finishing time: 10 minutes
Serves 6–8

margarine or butter, for greasing
¾ cup fine graham cracker crumbs
4 tablespoons margarine or butter, melted

FILLING AND TOPPING
1¼ cup milk
4 oz dark chocolate, broken into pieces
½ cup granulated sugar
3 tablespoons all-purpose flour
4 tablespoons margarine or butter
2 large egg yolks, lightly beaten
generous ½ cup heavy cream
1 piece candied ginger, finely chopped, grated orange rind, or chocolate, to decorate

1 Grease a 7–8 inch loose-bottomed pie pan. Mix the cracker crumbs with the margarine or butter until evenly coated.

2 Spoon the mixture into the pan and press it down evenly over the base and up the sides with the back of a metal spoon or an empty jar. Cover and refrigerate for 30 minutes.

3 Make the chocolate filling: Put the milk and chocolate into a heavy saucepan and heat gently, stirring frequently, until the chocolate has melted. Remove from the heat.

4 Combine the sugar, flour, margarine or butter and beaten egg yolks in a bowl and mix together thoroughly with a fork. Stir in the hot chocolate milk. Return the mixture to the pan and bring slowly to a boil, stirring constantly. Reduce the heat and cook, stirring constantly, for about 5 minutes until very thick and smooth.

5 Remove the pan from the heat and let the mixture cool for 5 minutes before pouring it into the crumb-coated pan. Leave for about 30 minutes until the filling is set.

6 Remove the pie from the pan and place it on a serving plate. Whip the cream until thick, then spread it generously over the top. Decorate with the chopped ginger, orange rind or chocolate, whichever you prefer. Refrigerate until required.

CHOCOLATE ECLAIRS

Preparation time: 20 minutes
Baking time: 40 minutes
Cooling time: 30–40 minutes
Finishing time: 25 minutes
Makes 8

vegetable oil and flour, for greasing
4 oz package of choux pastry mix

FILLING AND ICING
generous ½ cup whipping cream
2 drops vanilla extract
1 tablespoon granulated sugar
2 oz semi-sweet chocolate, broken into pieces
pat of butter
1 cup confectioner's sugar

1 Preheat the oven to 400F. Brush a large cookie sheet lightly with oil, then dust it with sifted flour. Using the handle of a wooden spoon, or a finger, mark 4 inches long lines on the cookie sheet, 1½ inches apart.

2 Put the pastry mix into a small bowl, add 1 cup tepid water and beat for 4 minutes. Put the paste in a piping bag fitted with a ¾ inch plain nozzle, and pipe on to the prepared cookie sheet. Holding the bag at an angle of 45° to the cookie sheet pipe the paste along the guidelines. Raise the nozzle at the end of each line and cut off the paste cleanly with a kitchen knife.

3 Bake in the oven for 40 minutes, until puffed and golden. With a palette knife, ease the éclairs off the cookie sheet and transfer to a wire rack. Split each one in half lengthways with a sharp knife, then scrape out and discard any uncooked pastry from the inside with a teaspoon. Leave to cool completely.

4 Make the filling: Whip the cream until it begins to thicken, then add the vanilla extract and sugar and continue beating until the mixture is thick but not stiff. Pipe or spoon the cream into the bottom half of each éclair, then replace the tops.

5 Make the icing: Put the chocolate, butter and 1 tablespoon water in a bowl over a pan half-full of simmering water. Leave, stirring occasionally, until the chocolate has melted. Remove the bowl from the pan and beat in the sifted confectioner's sugar, a little at a time. If necessary, beat in 1–2 more tablespoons of water to thin the icing to a spreading consistency.

6 Spoon or spread the icing over the tops of the éclairs, then leave in a cool place to set. Serve as soon as possible.

PROFITEROLES

Preparation time: 40 minutes
Cooling time: 30 minutes
Assembly time: 5 minutes
Makes 22

1½ cups unbleached, all-purpose flour
2 teaspoons granulated sugar
1 stick slightly salted butter, cut into small pieces
4 eggs
1 teaspoon brandy, rum or orange flower water (optional)
3¾ cups double cream
beaten egg and sugar, to glaze

CHOCOLATE SAUCE
9 oz semi-sweet chocolate
1 cup plus 2 tablespoons milk
piece of vanilla bean
2 tablespoons heavy cream
3 tablespoons butter
¼ cup granulated sugar

1 Preheat the oven to 400F

2 Sift the flour and sugar twice, then sift on to a sheet of waxed paper. (Unbleached all-purpose flour is preferable because its higher gluten content gives volume and crispness.) Set aside.

3 Put 1 cup plus 2 tablespoons water into a deep saucepan and add the butter. Place the pan over low heat and warm gently until all the butter has melted, then increase the heat to bring the liquid to a rolling boil. Draw the pan aside immediately and shoot in the flour mixture all at once. Lower the heat and return the pan to the stove immediately. Then, using a large wooden spoon, beat the paste vigorously until the flour has cooked and the mixture is smooth. It must not look grainy and should roll cleanly off the sides of the pan into a ball, leaving a floury film over the base. (The pastry mixture only takes a few seconds to cook before it forms into a ball. If allowed to cook too long the finished profiteroles will be heavy.) Remove from the heat and leave to cool for 5 minutes.

4 Break 1 egg into a cup and beat lightly with a fork, then pour onto the flour paste and beat thoroughly to blend. Continue in the same way with the remaining eggs, adding only a little at a time towards the end, so the mixture does not get too moist (you may even need a little more egg if conditions are very dry). If the choux mixture is too moist it will fail to rise properly and be inclined to spread. The finished paste should be quite firm but elastic – it will drop from a spoon slowly when jerked. Beat the paste well until it is shiny and smooth. Beat in brandy, rum or orange flower water if desired.

5 Chill a flat cookie sheet: hold it under cold running water for a few moments, shake off excess moisture but leave damp. Place teaspoonfuls of the mixture, about 1 inch in size, at 2 inch intervals on the wet sheet to allow the profiteroles room to expand. Lightly brush a little beaten egg on each one and sprinkle a pinch of sugar over the top to glaze.

6 Place the cookie sheet in the oven. Choux pastry buns can burn very easily so it is important that the oven temperature is correct. If your oven is inclined to overheat, use a layer of foil on top of the cookie sheet or slide a second cookie sheet underneath for added protection while cooking. Bake for about 20 minutes until the profiteroles are well browned all over and feel very light and hollow when picked up. Do not open the oven door until the buns have cooked for at least 15 minutes. If not cooked sufficiently, the delicate buns may collapse.

7 Remove the sheet from the oven. Pierce each bun with a skewer or knife to release the steam inside. Leave to cool on a wire rack.

8 Meanwhile, make the chocolate sauce: Melt the chocolate (see page 9).

9 Pour the milk into a separate saucepan and add the vanilla bean. Bring to a boil, then add 2 tablespoons of cream and bring back to a boil. Lift the pan off the heat, remove the vanilla bean, then stir in the melted chocolate, butter and sugar. Return to the heat and boil for a few seconds, stirring until thickened.

10 Whip 3⅛ cups of cream until stiff. Cut each profiterole in half and scoop a spoonful of whipped cream into each one. Replace the tops.

11 Pile the filled profiteroles attractively onto a glass or china serving plate. Pour over the hot chocolate sauce and serve at once.

CHOCOLATE CHIFFON PIE

Preparation time: 35 minutes
Chilling time: 45 minutes
Finishing time: 20 minutes
Setting time: 3 hours
Serves 6

1½ cup Brazil nuts
2 tablespoons granulated sugar

FILLING
1 tablespoon gelatine
½ cup granulated sugar
¼ teaspoon salt
1 cup milk
2 eggs separated
8 oz semi-sweet chocolate, broken into pieces
1 teaspoon vanilla extract
1¼ cups whipped cream
2 tablespoons chopped Brazil nuts, to decorate

1 Preheat the oven to 400F.

2 Grind the Brazil nuts in a food mill or blender. Blend the ground nuts and the sugar thoroughly, using the back of a spoon or the blender.

3 With your fingers, press the mixture into the bottom and around the sides of a 9 inch tart dish. Place the dish in the oven and bake for 8–10 minutes, or until the crust is lightly browned. Remove from the oven and leave to cool.

4 Make the filling: Put the gelatine, half the sugar and the salt in the top of a double boiler. With a wooden spoon, stir in the milk, egg yolks and chocolate.

5 Stirring continuously, cook for 6 minutes or until the gelatine has dissolved and the chocolate melted. Remove from the heat and beat until well blended. Stir in the vanilla extract and chill for about 45 minutes.

6 Remove the chocolate mixture from the refrigerator. It should be just on the point of setting. With a metal spoon, fold in 1 cup of the cream.

7 Beat the egg whites until they are almost stiff. Add 2 teaspoons of the remaining sugar and continue to beat until the whites form peaks. Using a metal spoon, fold in the remaining sugar. Carefully fold the beaten egg whites into the chilled chocolate mixture. Pour the filling into the pie shell and chill for 3 hours or until firm.

8 Decorate with the remaining whipped cream and the chopped Brazil nuts just before serving.

CHOCOLATE BAKEWELL

Preparation time: 1 hour
Baking time: 30 minutes
Serves 6–8

shortcrust pastry for a 9 inch crust, defrosted if frozen
1–2 tablespoons jam
milk, for glazing

CHOCOLATE FILLING
1 stick butter, diced
½ cup granulated sugar
¾ cup ground rice
2 tablespoons ground almonds
1 tablespoon cocoa powder, sifted
1 egg, lightly beaten
½ teaspoon almond extract

1. On a lightly floured surface, roll out the pastry and use to line a 9 inch fluted metal pie dish with a loose-bottomed base. Wrap pastry trimmings in plastic wrap and reserve. Prick base of pastry crust with a fork very thoroughly, and refrigerate.

2. Meanwhile, preheat the oven to 400F. Melt the butter in a heavy saucepan over low heat. Remove from the heat and stir in the sugar. Add the ground rice, almonds and cocoa powder, mix thoroughly, and then beat in the egg and extract. Leave the mixture to cool completely.

3. Knead the reserved pastry trimmings lightly together, then roll out into a 9 inch length and cut this into 6 narrow strips.

4. Spread the jam over the base of the pastry crust, then spread the cold chocolate mixture evenly over the jam.

5. Brush the pastry strips on both sides lightly with milk. Twist each strip to make a corkscrew shape and arrange on top of the tart in a lattice pattern, pressing the ends onto the pastry edge to seal.

6. Bake for about 30 minutes, until the chocolate filling is springy to the touch. Cool the bakewell for a few minutes, then remove the pan sides and slide the pie out on to a wire rack. Serve warm or cold.

CHOCOLATE CHERRY TART

Preparation time: 45 minutes
Chilling time: 30 minutes
Baking time: 30 minutes
Serves 4–6

1¾ cups all-purpose flour
⅛ teaspoon salt
1 tablespoon granulated sugar
3 tablespoons butter
3 tablespoons shortening
1 egg yolk, lightly beaten with ½ tablespoon water

FILLING
6 tablespoons butter
⅓ cup granulated sugar
2 large eggs, lightly beaten
¾ cup flour, sifted with ½ teaspoon baking powder
2 tablespoons cocoa powder
½ cup ground almonds
½ teaspoon almond extract
grated rind of 1 lemon
2 tablespoons black cherry jam

1 Preheat the oven to 375F.

2 Sift the flour and salt into a bowl. Stir in the sugar. Cut the butter and shortening into small pieces. Rub the fat into the flour until the mixture resembles fine bread crumbs. Make a well and add the egg yolk and 1 tablespoon ice water. Mix with a knife, then knead the pastry until smooth. Add more ice water if the pastry is too dry.

3 Pat the pastry into a ball, then roll out. Line a 7 inch tart dish with the pastry, trimming off any overlapping edges. Chill for 30 minutes. Reserve the trimmings.

4 Meanwhile, make the filling: Cream the butter with the back of a wooden spoon. Gradually beat in the sugar until the mixture is light and fluffy. Beat in the eggs. Lightly fold in the flour, cocoa, ground almonds, almond extract and lemon rind.

5 Remove the pastry-lined dish from the refrigerator. Spread the jam evenly over the bottom. Spoon in the cocoa mixture. Roll the trimmings into thin strips. Twist and arrange them in a lattice on the top.

6 Bake for 30 minutes, or until the filling is firm to the touch.

CHOCOLATE BRIOCHES

Preparation time: 2¾ hours
Chilling time: overnight
Baking time: 12 minutes
Cooling time: 30 minutes
Makes 40

4½ cups unbleached flour
4 tablespoons granulated sugar
½ teaspoon salt
2 tablespoons active dry yeast
4 eggs
1 cup lukewarm milk
1 teaspoon vanilla extract
1 stick butter, softened
flour, for kneading
3–4 oz thin dark chocolate bar
butter, for greasing
beaten egg, to glaze

1 Sift the flour, sugar and salt into a warmed bowl, sprinkle in the yeast and make a well.

2 Beat the eggs with the milk and vanilla and add to the flour. Mix well with one hand. Add half the butter in small pieces, and beat with one hand for 5–10 minutes until the dough is soft. Dot dough with the remaining butter; cover with plastic wrap and leave in a warm place for 1½ hours, until doubled in bulk.

3 Beat the dough vigorously with one hand for 5 minutes, or until it no longer sticks to the bowl. Cover bowl tightly with plastic wrap and chill overnight.

4 Next day, cut the chocolate into fingers with a sharp knife. Dip the blade in boiling water every few minutes.

5 Roll out the brioche dough to ¼ inch thick and cut it into 2 inch squares. Place a finger of chocolate in the center of each square. Roll dough to enclose the chocolate. Place the rolls on a greased baking sheet. Leave in warm place for 30 minutes, until doubled in bulk.

6 Preheat the oven to 400F. Brush the brioche rolls lightly with beaten egg and bake in the oven for 12 minutes. Cool on wire racks and serve.

CAKES AND GATEAUX

Chocolate and sponge cake is a combination made in heaven – and you'll find enough delights here to tempt an angel! From the classics of *haute cuisine* like Sachertorte and Black Forest Layer Cherry Cake to family favorites like Chocolate Cookie Cake and Chocolate Cream Log, clear instructions and inspiring illustrations ensure success every time.

CHOCOLATE PEPPERMINT GATEAU

Preparation time: 30 minutes
Baking time: 1–1¼ hours
Finishing time: 30 minutes
Serves 20

margarine, for greasing
4 oz semi-sweet chocolate
1¼ cups milk
1 cup light soft brown sugar, firmly packed
⅓ cup soft margarine
2 eggs, separated
2¼ cups all-purpose flour
1 teaspoon baking soda

ICING AND DECORATION
⅓ cup margarine or butter, softened
1 cup confectioner's sugar, sifted
few drops of green food coloring
few drops of peppermint extract
⅓ cup chocolate sprinkles
4 wafer-thin peppermint chocolates, cut diagonally in half
1 oz semi-sweet chocolate, grated

1 Preheat the oven to 325F. Grease a deep 8 inch square cake pan and line with waxed paper.

2 Break the chocolate into a small bowl set over a pan of simmering water. Add half the milk and half the sugar. Do not stir until the chocolate has almost melted. Then remove from the heat, gently stir in the remaining milk and mix well.

3 Beat the fat and remaining sugar with the egg yolks. Beat in the chocolate mixture, then sift in the flour and baking soda. Mix until well blended, then beat for 1 minute.

4 In a clean dry bowl, beat the egg whites until standing in stiff peaks. Then, using a metal spoon, carefully fold the egg whites into the mixture, 1 tablespoon at a time.

5 Turn the mixture into the prepared pan and smooth the top with a palette knife. Bake for 1–1¼ hours, until the cake springs back when lightly pressed. Turn onto a wire rack, remove the lining paper, turn the cake the right way up and leave to cool.

6 Meanwhile, make peppermint icing: Beat the margarine or butter until it is soft and creamy. Gradually beat in the confectioner's sugar, green coloring, peppermint extract and enough water to make a smooth butter cream which will hold its shape when fluffed with a fork.

7 Spread one-third of the icing around the sides of the cake. Spread the sprinkles out on a piece of waxed paper then, holding the cake firmly in both hands, dip the sides in the sprinkles until they are completely coated.

8 Put the cake on a serving plate. Spread half the remaining icing over the top of the cake then, using a piping bag with a large rosette nozzle, pipe the rest in a border around the edge of the cake. Arrange the peppermint chocolate halves in the piped icing and then sprinkle the grated chocolate over the center.

CHOCOLATE RUM CAKE

Preparation time: 25 minutes
Baking time: 65 minutes
Cooling time: 40 minutes
Softening time: 24 hours
Serves 6–8

- vegetable oil, for greasing
- 1 cup plus 2 tablespoons flour
- ½ teaspoon baking powder
- ½ teaspoon baking soda
- 3 tablespoons cocoa powder
- 2 tablespoons dark rum
- 1 stick margarine or butter, softened
- 1 cup granulated sugar
- 2 eggs, beaten
- ½ cup ground almonds

TOPPING

- ¾ cup whipping cream
- 1 tablespoon superfine sugar
- 2 drops vanilla extract
- 1 egg white, stiffly beaten

1 Preheat the oven to 325F. Grease a deep 7 inch round pan with a loose-bottomed base. Line the base with greased waxed paper.

2 Sift the flour with the baking soda and baking powder. Put the cocoa powder into a small bowl and gradually blend in the rum and ⅜ cup plus 1 tablespoon cold water.

3 Beat the margarine or butter and sugar together until pale and fluffy. Add the eggs, a little at a time, beating vigorously after each addition. Using a large metal spoon, stir in the cocoa mixture, ground almonds and sifted flour, in alternate spoonfuls.

4 Turn the mixture into the prepared pan and level the surface. Bake in the oven for about 65 minutes, until the cake is springy to the touch.

5 Cool the cake for 10 minutes, then run a palette knife around the sides and remove from the pan. Carefully peel off the lining paper. Leave the cake on a wire rack to cool completely. Wrap and store for 24 hours before cutting to allow the texture to become soft and moist.

6 Just before serving, make the topping: whip the cream until it begins to thicken, then add the sugar (adjust to taste) and vanilla. Beat until the cream just holds its shape. Fold in the egg white and serve at once, putting a generous spoonful of flavored cream on each slice.

SACHERTORTE

Preparation time: 40 minutes
Baking time: 1 hour
Cooling time: 2 hours
Finishing time: 30 minutes
Setting time: 2–3 hours
Serves 12

melted butter, for greasing
6 oz semi-sweet chocolate, broken into pieces
1½ sticks butter, softened
1 cup confectioner's sugar, sifted
6 eggs, separated
2–3 drops vanilla extract
1½ cups all-purpose flour, sifted
8 tablespoons apricot jam

ICING
5 oz semi-sweet chocolate, broken into pieces
½ cup confectioner's sugar, sifted
2½ teaspoons glycerine

1 Preheat the oven to 350F. Line a loose-bottomed, deep 9 inch round cake pan with waxed paper. Grease the paper.

2 Melt the chocolate (see page 9). Set aside.

3 Beat the butter until creamy. Add ½ cup plus 2 tablespoons confectioner's sugar; beat until pale and fluffy. Gradually beat in the egg yolks, then the melted chocolate and the vanilla extract.

4 Beat the egg whites until they stand in soft peaks. Beat in the remaining confectioner's sugar and continue beating until the mixture is stiff. Using a large metal spoon, lightly fold the beaten egg whites into the chocolate mixture, alternating with the flour (2 tablespoons at a time).

5 Pour the mixture into the prepared pan and make a shallow hollow in the center. Bake for 50–60 minutes, until a warmed skewer inserted into the center comes out clean.

6 Leave to cool in the pan for 5 minutes, then turn out on a wire rack. Carefully peel off the lining paper; turn the right way up and leave to cool for at least 2 hours, preferably overnight.

7 Cut the cold cake horizontally in half. (Use a sharp knife with a serrated edge and cut with a sawing action.) Next, strain the jam into a small saucepan; warm very gently until melted. Then remove it from the heat.

8 Place the top half of the cake, cut side uppermost, on a wire rack and spread with half the jam. Place the other half on top. Spread the top and sides with the rest of the jam.

9 Make the icing: Heat the chocolate and 5 tablespoons of water in a small bowl over a pan of simmering water, stirring occasionally, until the chocolate has just melted. Remove from the heat and, using a balloon whisk, beat in the confectioner's sugar and glycerine until the mixture is smooth.

10 Pour the icing over the cake and allow it to run down the sides. If necessary, dip a palette knife in hot water and use it to smooth the icing and give an even coating.

11 Leave the cake in a cool place for 2–3 hours until the icing has set. Do not chill or freeze as this will spoil the gloss. It is traditional to pipe the word "Sacher" across the set top.

12 Served with whipped cream.

CHOCOLATE NOUGAT CAKE

Preparation time: 30 minutes
Chilling time: 3 hours
Serves 8–10

- **generous ¾ cup sweet unsalted butter, softened**
- **bare 1 cup granulated sugar**
- **½ cup cocoa powder, sifted**
- **1 egg**
- **1 egg yolk**
- **½ cup crushed vanilla wafers**
- **½ cup almonds, blanched, peeled and chopped**
- **2 tablespoons brandy**
- **oil for greasing**
- **¾ cup whipped cream, to decorate**
- **candied flowers or other cake decorations**

1 Beat the softened butter and sugar together until creamy. Add the sifted cocoa and mix it well into the butter cream.

2 Beat the egg and the yolk together and beat them into the cocoa mixture.

3 Add the cookie crumbs to the mixture with the chopped almonds. Mix well. Add the brandy and mix again very thoroughly.

4 Lightly oil a 9 inch cake pan and line it with waxed paper. Spoon the cookie crumb mixture into the pan, then press it down and flatten it with a palette knife or an empty jar. Refrigerate the mixture for at least 3 hours, until firm.

5 Turn this traditional Italian nougat cake out on to a round or oval dish and cover the top with whipped cream. Decorate with candied flowers or other cake decorations.

SWISS CHOCOLATE CREAM CAKE

Preparation time: 35 minutes
Chilling time: overnight
Finishing time: 10 minutes
Serves 6–8

4 oz semi-sweet chocolate
¾ cup milk
6 tablespoons butter
½ cup granulated sugar
1 egg yolk
1¼ cup whipping cream
24 lady fingers

DECORATION
¾ cup whipped cream, (optional)
chopped nuts or grated chocolate

1 Line a 9 × 5 × 3 inches loaf pan with foil or thick waxed paper, leaving a good border each side to lift out the cake.

2 Grate the chocolate coarsely. Melt the chocolate in half the milk in a saucepan over a low heat, removing it as soon as the chocolate is melted. Stir in the remainder of the milk and reserve.

3 Cream the butter and sugar together until they are light and creamy, beat in the egg yolk and then the chocolate mixture, and continue beating until the mixture is smooth. Whip the cream until it is thick.

4 Pour one-third of the chocolate mixture into the lined pan, cover with a layer of lady fingers, then a third of the whipped cream. Repeat twice to make a total of three layers, finishing with whipped cream. Chill overnight.

5 When ready to serve, turn the cake out on to an oblong serving plate. Cover the sides with the whipped cream, if liked, and decorate with some chopped nuts or grated chocolate. A scalloped border of whipped cream around the base and top of the cake makes this elegant dessert look even more splendid.

BLACK FOREST LAYER CAKE

Preparation time: 1½ hours
Cooling time: overnight
Finishing time: 1¾ hours
Serves 12–14

butter and flour for greasing
6½ oz dark chocolate, broken into pieces
bare 1 cup butter
7 egg whites
1¼ cups confectioner's sugar, sifted
1¾ cups all-purpose flour
1 teaspoon baking powder

FILLING AND DECORATION
2 cups whole black cherries, pitted
⅓ cup confectioner's sugar
2 tablespoons granulated sugar
few drops vanilla extract
1 cup Kirsch
2 cups heavy cream
¼ cup chocolate shavings

1 Preheat the oven to 350F. Butter and flour a deep 10 inch round cake pan. Melt the chocolate (see page 9).

2 Beat the butter until fluffy. Add the chocolate and beat.

3 Sift the baking powder into the flour. Beat the egg whites until stiff, then add the confectioner's sugar. Fold in the chocolate mixture and the flour. Bake in the center of the oven for 1 hour until springy to the touch. Cool in the pan for 5 minutes, then turn out onto a wire rack and leave to cool overnight.

4 Make the filling: Reserve 13 cherries for decoration and halve the rest. Place the cut fruit in a bowl; dust with 4 tablespoons confectioner's sugar and 1 tablespoon sugar. Add a drop of vanilla and pour over ½ cup Kirsch. Cover for 3–4 hours.

5 Pour off all the liquid from the cherries into a small saucepan; heat gently but do not allow to boil. Pour over the cherries and leave overnight.

6 Slice the cake into 3 horizontal layers. Pour off the cherry liquid and measure it. Reduce to ¾ cup over a low heat, then add ¼ cup Kirsch. Spoon over the cake; leave to soak for 30 minutes.

7 Whip the cream until stiff, add remaining confectioner's sugar, sugar, vanilla and Kirsch. Spread 1 cake layer with one-third of the cream and half the cut cherries. Put second cake layer on top and repeat. Add the third cake layer and cover the cake with cream. Decorate with whole cherries and shavings. Chill for at least 1 hour.

CHOCOLATE ALMOND CAKE

Preparation time: 40 minutes
Baking time: 30 minutes
Cooling time: 2 hours
Finishing time: 10 minutes
Serves 6–8

1 stick plus ½ tablespoon butter, softened
3 tablespoons all-purpose flour
4 oz semi-sweet baking chocolate
4 tablespoons rum or strong black coffee
½ cup plus 1 tablespoon granulated sugar
3 eggs, separated
⅛ teaspoon salt
½ cup ground almonds
¼ teaspoon almond extract
¼ cup slivered almonds, to decorate

ICING
2 oz semi-sweet chocolate
1 tablespoon rum or strong black coffee
4 tablespoons sweet unsalted butter

[1] Preheat the oven to 350F. Butter and flour a round 8 inch cake pan with ½ tablespoon of the butter and 1 tablespoon of the flour.

[2] Put the chocolate and the rum or coffee in a bowl over a pan of simmering water, stirring occasionally. As soon as the chocolate melts, remove from the heat.

[3] Put the remaining butter and the sugar in a medium-sized mixing bowl. Cream together with the back of a wooden spoon until light and creamy. Beat in the egg yolks and continue beating until the mixture is smooth and creamy.

[4] Put the egg whites and salt in another bowl and beat until they form soft peaks. Add the remaining sugar and beat until the whites are stiff.

[5] With a metal spoon, mix the melted chocolate into the egg yolk mixture. When thoroughly blended, stir in the ground almonds and the almond extract and mix well.

[6] Gently fold in half the beaten egg whites. When the mixture is almost blended, sift half the remaining flour on top of the mixture and, folding continuously, add the rest of the egg whites. Finally, fold in the remaining flour.

[7] Pour the mixture into the prepared pan and bake for 30 minutes or until a skewer comes out clean.

[8] Remove the cake from the oven and leave it to stand for 15 minutes. Then run a knife around the edge of the pan and turn the cake onto a wire rack. Leave it to cool for 2 hours.

[9] Meanwhile make the icing: Melt the chocolate in the rum or coffee, as before. As soon as the chocolate melts remove from the heat.

[10] With a wooden spoon, gradually beat in the butter. When all the butter has been added, place the bowl over a basin of ice water and beat until the icing is cool and has thickened to a spreading consistency.

[11] Cover the cake with the icing, smoothing it on evenly with a knife. Decorate the top with the slivered almonds.

CHOCOLATE MARBLE CAKE

Preparation time: 30 minutes
Baking time: 50 minutes
Cooling time: 2–3 hours
Serves 10

¾ cup margarine or butter, softened
2 tablespoons ground almonds
¾ cup granulated sugar
3 eggs, lightly beaten
¾ cup all-purpose flour
1 teaspoon baking powder
1 tablespoon cocoa powder
1 tablespoon vanilla extract

1 Preheat the oven to 350F.

2 Butter a 9 × 5 × 3 inches loaf pan, then coat with the almonds.

3 Beat 12 tablespoons margarine or butter and the sugar until pale and fluffy. Add the eggs a little at a time, beating thoroughly after each addition. Sift the flour and the baking powder together and fold into the mixture with a large metal spoon.

4 Divide the mixture in half. Sift the cocoa into one half and lightly fold it in, then stir the vanilla into the other half.

5 Spread half the vanilla mixture in the prepared pan and level the surface. Cover with half the cocoa mixture. Repeat this process to make two more layers.

6 Bake for about 50 minutes, until a warmed, fine skewer inserted into the center comes out clean. (Cover the pan with waxed paper after 30 minutes' baking time to prevent the top of the cake overbrowning.)

7 Cool the cake for 2-3 minutes then run a palette knife around the sides and very carefully turn it out of the pan. Turn the right way up and leave on a wire rack to cool completely before slicing and serving. The cake will keep fresh for up to 1 week in an airtight container.

MOCHA LAYER CAKE

Preparation time: 15 minutes
Baking time: 25–30 minutes
Cooling time: 2–3 hours
Assembly time: 25 minutes
Serves 8–10

vegetable oil, for greasing
2 cups all-purpose flour
2 tablespoons cocoa powder
3 teaspoons baking powder
1 cup soft margarine
1 cup dark soft brown sugar, firmly packed
4 large eggs, lightly beaten

FILLING AND TOPPING
1 cup confectioner's sugar, plus 1 teaspoon
2½ teaspoons coffee and chicory extract
½-¾ cup heavy cream
chocolate cake decorations

[1] Preheat the oven to 325F. Grease 2 shallow 7 inch square pans, line the bases with waxed paper, then grease the paper.

[2] Sift the flour, cocoa and baking powder into a large bowl. Add the margarine, sugar and eggs and beat with a wooden spoon for 2–3 minutes, until evenly blended.

[3] Divide the mixture equally between the pans, level each surface, then make a shallow hollow in the center. Bake for 25–30 minutes, or until springy to the touch.

[4] Cool for 5 minutes, then turn out onto a wire rack and peel off the lining papers. Turn the cakes the right way and leave to cool completely.

[5] Assemble the cake: Sift ¾ cup confectioner's sugar into a bowl, add 1½ teaspoons coffee and chicory extract, then stir in enough warm water to give a smooth icing that just coats the back of the spoon. Spread half the icing over each layer.

[6] Whip the cream until thickened. Add the remaining extract and confectioner's sugar. Beat until soft peaks form.

[7] Spread one-quarter of the coffee cream over 1 iced layer, then place the other layer on top. Lift the layers gently as the icing cracks easily. Pipe the remaining coffee cream around the top edge of the cake, then decorate with chocolate cake decorations.

BLACK AND WHITE CHOCOLATE LAYER CAKE

Preparation time: 1 hour
Baking time: 4½ hours
Cooling time: 2 hours
Finishing time: 30 minutes
Serves 8–10

MERINGUE LAYER
vegetable oil, for greasing
2 egg whites
pinch of salt
½ cup granulated sugar
½ teaspoon cornstarch
½ teaspoon white vinegar

CHOCOLATE LAYER
vegetable oil, for greasing
1 stick butter, softened
1 cup plus 2 tablespoons granulated sugar
2 egg yolks
1 egg
2¼ cups all-purpose flour
1 teaspoon baking soda
¼ cup cocoa powder
1 cup red wine

FILLING AND DECORATION
8 oz semi-sweet chocolate
8 oz white chocolate
6 tablespoons raspberry jam
2½ cups heavy cream
confectioner's sugar and cocoa powder, to decorate

1 Preheat the oven to 200F. Line a cookie sheet with waxed paper marked with a 9 inch circle, then grease the paper.

2 Make the meringue: Beat the egg whites and salt until stiff. Reserve 1 tablespoon granulated sugar and beat the remainder, 1 tablespoon at a time, into the egg whites, beating well between each addition, until the meringue is stiff and glossy.

3 Add the cornstarch to the reserved sugar and beat the mixture into the meringue. Stir in the vinegar with a metal spoon. The mixture should now stand in very stiff peaks.

4 Spread the meringue evenly onto the marked circle on the cookie sheet. Bake for about 4 hours until completely dry and crisp. Leave to cool on the paper. When completely cold, peel off the paper, then store in an airtight tin until required.

5 Preheat the oven to 350F. Brush the bases of two 9½ inch cake pans with oil, line with circles of waxed paper, then oil the paper.

6 Make the chocolate cake: Cream the butter and half the sugar together until light and fluffy. Add the remaining sugar and beat well again.

7 Add the egg yolks and the whole egg, one at a time, beating well after each addition, until the mixture is thoroughly combined.

8 Sift together the flour, baking soda and cocoa powder and fold lightly into the creamed mixture, alternately with the red wine, beginning and ending with the flour and cocoa mixture.

9 Divide the mixture equally between the 2 prepared pans and level the surfaces. Bake in the oven for 25 minutes, or until the cakes feel just firm to the touch. Leave to cool slightly in the pans, then turn the cakes out onto wire racks. Remove the lining papers and leave until cold.

10 Meanwhile, use the semi-sweet chocolate to make caraque and the white chocolate to make curls (see page 10). Chill until required.

11 To assemble the cake, split the 2 layers in half horizontally and spread the base of each with raspberry jam. Sandwich the layers together again.

12 Whip the cream until stiff. Place one chocolate layer on a serving plate and spread with one-quarter of the whipped cream. Top with the meringue layer and spread with another quarter of the cream. Top with the second chocolate layer. Trim the edges of the meringue, if necessary.

13 Spread the remaining cream over the top and sides of the cake. Lightly press the semi-sweet chocolate caraque on to the sides using a palette knife.

14 Arrange the white chocolate curls on the top of the cake and sprinkle with sifted confectioner's sugar and cocoa powder. Chill until required.

Illustrated on page 31.

CHOCOLATE AND SOUR CREAM CAKE

Preparation time: 25 minutes
Baking time: 15–20 minutes
Finishing time: 30–40 minutes
Serves 6–8

¾ cups butter
5½ cups all-purpose flour, sifted
7 oz unsweetened chocolate
1 cup plus 2 tablespoons granulated sugar
4 eggs
1 teaspoon vanilla extract
1½ teaspoons baking powder
¼ teaspoon salt
1 cup milk

ICING
24 oz semi-sweet chocolate, broken into pieces
¼ teaspoon salt
2 cups sour cream
12 walnuts, shelled and halved

1 With 1 tablespoon butter and 2 tablespoons of flour lightly coat two 9 inch square, deep cake pan. Preheat the oven to 375F.

2 Melt the chocolate (see page 9) and set aside.

3 Cream the remaining butter and the sugar until light and fluffy. Beat in the eggs, one at a time. Beat in the melted chocolate and the vanilla.

4 Sift the remaining flour, the baking powder and the salt together and beat half into the chocolate mixture, then add half the milk and mix well. Beat in the remaining seasoned flour. When well mixed, add the rest of the milk. Beat the mixture until smooth.

5 Pour an equal amount of mixture into each pan. Bake in the center of the oven for 15–20 minutes or until a skewer inserted into the center comes out clean. Then run a knife around the edge of each cake and invert them onto a wire rack. Leave to cool.

6 Meanwhile make the icing: Melt the chocolate as before. As soon as it has melted stir in the salt and sour cream. Set aside for 20 minutes or until it cools to room temperature and thickens to a spreading consistency.

7 Sandwich the layers with icing and then cover the top and sides, using a palette knife. Decorate the top with the walnut halves.

CHOCOLATE NUT TORTE

Preparation time: 1¼ hours
Baking time: 20–25 minutes
Cooling time: 2 hours
Finishing time: 30 minutes
Chilling time: 1 hour
Serves 8

7 eggs, separated
1 cup granulated sugar
1 teaspoon vanilla extract
1 cup ground hazelnuts
1 cup ground pecans
1 tablespoon bread crumbs
1 teaspoon baking powder
½ teaspoon salt

WHIPPED CREAM FILLING
1 cup heavy cream
2 tablespoons confectioner's sugar
1 teaspoon vanilla extract
1–2 tablespoons brandy (optional)

DARK CHOCOLATE FROSTING
6 tablespoons margarine or butter
4 oz semi-sweet chocolate, melted and cooled (see page 9)
2 teaspoons vanilla extract
2¼ cups confectioner's sugar, sifted
1 tablespoon instant coffee dissolved in 2 tablespoons hot water, light cream or milk
whole hazelnuts or pecans, to decorate

1 Place the egg whites in a bowl; let stand at room temperature for 1 hour. Grease three 8 inch cake pans lightly and line with greased waxed paper. Heat the oven to 375F.

2 Beat the egg yolks for 5–6 minutes, until thick and lemon-colored. Beat in the sugar gradually until very thick. Add the vanilla and beat. Combine the ground nuts, bread crumbs, baking powder and salt; fold into the egg yolk mixture.

3 Beat the egg whites until stiff. Stir half into the egg and nut mixture, then fold in the rest.

4 Divide the mixture equally among the pans and smooth the tops. Bake for 20–25 minutes until springy. Cool in pans on wire racks for 5 minutes. Turn over onto racks covered with waxed paper. Remove pans and peel off lining paper. Allow to cool completely.

5 Whip the cream until thick. Add the icing sugar and vanilla; beat until stiff. Beat in the brandy, if using. Chill.

6 Beat the butter in a bowl until very smooth. Beat in the melted chocolate and vanilla until well mixed. Beat in the confectioner's sugar. Add the dissolved coffee, 1 tablespoon at a time, beating until the frosting is a smooth spreading consistency.

7 Trim any crusty edges from the cake. Sandwich the 3 layers with whipped cream. Spread frosting around the sides and over the top with a long, flat rubber spatula. Spoon the remaining frosting into a piping bag fitted with a rosette nozzle; pipe rosettes around the top edge of the cake. Decorate each rosette with a whole hazelnut or pecan half. Refrigerate for at least 1 hour before serving.

FUDGEY DEVIL'S FOOD CAKE

Preparation time: 25 minutes
Baking time: 25–30 minutes
Finishing time: 2 hours
Serves 8–10

butter and flour for pans
½ cup cocoa powder
½ tablespoon white vinegar or lemon juice
1¼ cups milk
2¾ cups all-purpose flour
2 teaspoons baking soda
½ teaspoon baking powder
1 teaspoon salt
1 cup or 2 sticks margarine or butter, softened
2 cups granulated sugar
2 teaspoons vanilla extract
4 eggs

CHOCOLATE BUTTER ICING
4 oz semi-sweet chocolate, broken into pieces
5 egg yolks
1 cup confectioner's sugar
3 sticks sweet butter, softened
1½ teaspoons vanilla extract
1 tablespoon instant coffee, dissolved in 2 tablespoons hot water (optional)

1 Preheat the oven to 350F. Grease and flour two 9 inch round cake pans.

2 Pour 1 cup boiling water over the cocoa and stir to dissolve. Set aside to cool. Make sour milk: Stir the vinegar or lemon juice into the milk and let stand at room temperature for 5 minutes.

3 Sift the flour, baking soda, baking powder and salt together and set aside. Beat the margarine or butter until smooth, add the sugar and beat until light and fluffy. Beat in the vanilla and the eggs, one at a time, beating well after each addition. Add the cooled cocoa and mix well.

4 Add the flour and sour milk, alternately. Beat until blended. Begin and end with flour.

5 Divide the mixture equally between the pans and smooth the tops. Bake for 25–30 minutes, until a warmed skewer inserted in the cake comes out clean.

6 Cool the cakes in the pans on wire racks for 10 minutes. Then turn out on to the racks and leave to cool completely.

7 Meanwhile, make the icing: Melt the chocolate (see page 9). Beat the egg yolks until pale yellow (about 5 minutes). Mix the sugar with ½ cup water in a heavy saucepan over low heat; stir until the sugar dissolves. Raise the heat and boil, without stirring, until the temperature reaches 110–112C/230–234F on a cooking thermometer (soft ball stage). Remove from heat. Pour the syrup in a thin, steady stream into the egg yolks, beating until the mixture is completely cool.

8 Beat the butter and vanilla until smooth and creamy. Gradually beat in the egg yolk mixture, then the melted chocolate and dissolved coffee (if using). Mix well and chill for 10–15 minutes.

9 Spread 1 layer, bottom side up, with about one-third of the icing. Add the second layer and ice the top and sides, using a thin icing spatula. The icing should be fairly thick. Chill until ready to serve.

CHOCOLATE COOKIE CAKE

Preparation time: 15 minutes
Chilling time: 8 hours
Serves 10–12

butter, for greasing
8 oz semi-sweet chocolate, broken into pieces
2 sticks sweet butter, diced
2 eggs
¼ cup granulated sugar
3 tablespoons candied peel
12 marashino cherries, rinsed, dried and quartered
¼ cup blanched almonds, chopped
1 teaspoon grated orange rind (omit if using coffee liqueur)
1 cup graham crackers, coarsely crushed
2–3 tablespoons Cointreau or coffee liqueur (optional)

[1] Butter a loose-bottomed, shallow 8 inch round pan. Line the base with waxed paper; butter the paper.

[2] Put the chocolate and butter into a bowl over a pan of barely simmering water. Heat gently until melted, then set aside to cool slightly.

[3] In a large bowl, beat the eggs and sugar with a wooden spoon until pale and frothy. Slowly stir in the melted chocolate mixture, then stir in the peel, cherries, almonds and orange rind if using.

[4] Add the crushed graham crackers and mix thoroughly, then stir in the Cointreau or coffee liqueur, if using. Turn the mixture into the prepared pan and level the top. Cover with plastic wrap and refrigerate for 8 hours.

[5] To serve: Uncover the cake and run a palette knife around the sides to loosen it. Remove the sides of the pan. Cut the cake into small wedges and serve at once, while still chilled.

CHOCOLATE CREAM LOG

Preparation time: 15 minutes
Baking time: 12–14 minutes
Finishing time: 40–50 minutes
Serves 8

vegetable oil, for greasing
a good ½ cup all-purpose flour
2 tablespoons cocoa powder
pinch of baking powder
3 large eggs
½ cup granulated sugar
extra granulated sugar

FILLING AND TOPPING
1¼ cups whipping cream
2 tablespoons orange-flavored liqueur (optional)
8 fancy chocolate candies, to decorate

1 Preheat the oven to 400F. Grease a 12 × 8 inch cookie sheet, line with waxed paper, then grease the paper. Sift the flour, cocoa and baking powder together and set aside.

2 Put the eggs and sugar into a large bowl. Set above a pan of gently simmering water. Beat until the mixture is thick enough to hold a trail for 3 seconds.

3 Remove the bowl from the heat and beat for a few minutes, then fold in the flour and 1 tablespoon hot water. Pour into the pan and spread evenly by gently tilting the pan. Bake immediately for 12–14 minutes, until well risen.

4 Lay a sheet of waxed paper on top of a clean, damp dish towel. Sprinkle the paper thickly with the sugar. Turn the baked cake out onto the sugared paper. Peel the lining paper off, then trim the crusty edges with a sharp knife. Make a shallow cut along 1 short end, about ½ inch from the edge. Roll up the cake with paper inside. Place seam-side down on a wire rack and leave to cool for 30 minutes.

5 Make the filling: Whip the cream, with the liqueur if using, until standing in soft peaks. Put one-quarter of the cream into a piping bag with a large star nozzle and reserve. Whip remaining cream until stiff.

6 Unroll the cake, remove paper and spread cake with cream, then roll up again.

7 Decorate with piped cream and chocolates. Serve on day of making.

CHOCOLATE AND COFFEE CAKE

Preparation time: 20 minutes
Baking time: 30 minutes
Cooling time: 2 hours
Finishing time: 20 minutes
Serves 6–8

butter and flour for the pan
¾ cup plus 2 tablespoons butter
bare 1 cup granulated sugar
4 eggs, beaten
2 cups all-purpose flour sifted with 1 teaspoon baking powder
2 tablespoons cocoa powder
2 teaspoons instant coffee powder

BUTTER ICING
1 stick butter
¾ cup confectioner's sugar, sifted
2 tablespoons cocoa powder
1 teaspoon coffee extract
flaked almonds, to decorate

1 Preheat the oven to 375F. Butter and flour two 7 inch cake pans. If you are using non-stick pans, they need be greased only lightly.

2 Beat together the butter and sugar until light and fluffy. Beat in the eggs a little at a time. Beat the mixture very thoroughly to prevent it from curdling. If the mixture starts to look grainy instead of smooth and creamy, add a spoonful of the flour with the next addition of beaten egg and reduce the amount of egg added at one time.

3 Sift the flour with the cocoa and coffee powders and fold into the creamed mixture.

4 Divide the mixture between the prepared pans. Spread the mixture evenly in each pan, then make a hollow in the center of each to prevent the mixture peaking during baking.

5 Bake for 30 minutes or until the cakes are firm and a warmed skewer inserted into the center comes out clean. Cool for 5 minutes in the pans, then turn the cakes out onto wire racks. Allow them to cool completely before icing.

6 Meanwhile, make the butter icing: Beat the butter with the sugar until light and fluffy. Dissolve the cocoa powder and coffee extract in 2 tablespoons boiling water and beat them into the butter until the icing is a smooth spreading consistency.

7 Use a long-bladed knife with a sharp serrated edge, cutting with a sawing action, to trim the top of the bottom layer so that it is level. Spread the bottom layer generously with half of the butter icing, then place the other layer on top and spread it with the remaining icing. The icing should stand in rough peaks.

8 Just before serving, decorate the cake with flaked almonds scattered across the top.

9 To store: Before filling wrap each layer in heavy-duty foil or plastic wrap and freeze for up to 6 months; defrost in the wrappings at room temperature for about 2 hours. Finish, ice and decorate the cake just before serving.

CHOKLADKAKA

Preparation time: 40 minutes
Baking time: 50 minutes
Cooling time: 1 hour
Serves 6–8

6 tablespoons butter
2 tablespoons dry white bread crumbs
¾ cup granulated sugar
2 eggs, separated
1 teaspoon vanilla extract
1½ cups all-purpose flour, sifted
1 teaspoon baking powder
3 oz milk chocolate, melted **(see page 9)**
½ cup light cream

1 Preheat the oven to 300F.

2 Grease a deep, 8 inch round cake pan. Sprinkle the bread crumbs into the pan and press them onto the bottom and sides of the pan so that it is completely lined. Set aside.

3 Cream the remaining butter with the back of a wooden spoon. Gradually beat in the sugar until the mixture is light and fluffy. Then beat in the egg yolks, one at a time, and add the vanilla extract.

4 Sift ¼ cup of the flour with the baking powder into the butter-and-sugar mixture and beat well. Blend in one-third of the melted chocolate and cream and add another ¼ cup of the flour. Continue adding the chocolate, cream and flour until all of it has been incorporated.

5 In another bowl, beat the egg whites until they form stiff peaks. With a metal spoon, gently fold the egg whites into the chocolate mixture.

6 Pour the mixture into the pan and bake for 50 minutes or until a skewer inserted in the center comes out clean. Turn the cake out of the pan onto a cake rack to cool.

7 Serve with or without whipped cream.

CHOCOLATE-MARMALADE RING

Preparation time: 40 minutes
Baking time: 40–45 minutes
Cooling time: 1–2 hours
Finishing time: 10 minutes
Serves 12–16

butter, for greasing
6 oz semi-sweet chocolate, melted
2¼ cups all-purpose flour
1 teaspoon baking powder
½ teaspoon baking soda
¼ teaspoon salt
¾ cup margarine or butter
1 cup granulated sugar
5 eggs, separated
⅜ cup orange marmalade
¾ cup milk
6 tablespoons ground almonds

CHOCOLATE CUSTARD FILLING
3 oz semi-sweet chocolate pieces
4 tablespoons margarine or butter
2 eggs, lightly beaten

1 Preheat the oven to 375F. Grease one 10 inch bundt pan.

2 Sift the flour, baking powder, baking soda and salt together.

3 Beat the butter until very smooth. Add the sugar and beat until light and fluffy. Beat in the egg yolks, one at a time, beating well after each addition. Stir in the melted chocolate and marmalade. Fold in the flour alternately with the milk.

4 Beat the egg whites until stiff. Stir 2 tablespoons into the mixture, then fold in the remaining whites and almonds.

5 Pour into the mold. Bake for 40-45 minutes or until springy. Cool the cake in the pan on a wire rack for 15 minutes, then turn out and cool.

6 Make the filling: Melt the chocolate and butter in the top of a double boiler, stirring constantly until smooth. Remove from heat and cool slightly. Beat in the eggs. Return the pan to heat; cook, beating constantly, for 2-3 minutes or until slightly thickened. Remove from heat and allow to cool.

7 If you want to frost the cake, make up 1½ quantities of Chocolate Butter Cream frosting or Crème au Beurre (see page 13). Add 3-4 tablespoons strong black coffee and a little extra sugar for Mocha frosting.

8 Cut the cake horizontally into 2 layers. Sandwich with the filling and cover the top and sides with icing, if liked. Chill until ready to serve.

Desserts and Puddings

Always sumptuous, chocolate is the ideal dessert ingredient. Anyone with a sweet tooth will find plenty of ideas here for every occasion. Offer your dinner guests a striking Italian Zuccotto or the classic Chocolate Mousse Special and the compliments will flow. For hungry families, try Magic Chocolate Pudding or Chocolate Nutty Tapioca for a filling finale.

MAGIC CHOCOLATE PUDDING

Preparation time: 15 minutes
Baking time: 40 minutes
Serves 4

margarine, for greasing
¾ cup all-purpose flour sifted with 1 teaspoon baking powder
2 tablespoons cocoa powder
pinch of salt
1 stick margarine or butter, softened
½ cup granulated sugar
½ teaspoon vanilla extract
2 eggs, lightly beaten
1–2 tablespoons milk

SAUCE
½ cup light soft brown sugar, firmly packed
2 tablespoons cocoa powder

1 Preheat the oven to 375F. Lightly grease a 5 cup, fairly deep, ovenproof pie dish.

2 Sift the flour into a bowl with the cocoa powder and salt, then set aside.

3 Beat the margarine or butter and sugar together until pale and fluffy, then beat in the vanilla. Beat in the eggs, a little at a time, adding 1 tablespoon of the flour mixture with the last few additions of egg. Gradually stir in the remaining flour mixture and mix well, then add enough milk to give a smooth, dropping consistency.

4 Spoon the mixture into the prepared dish, spread it evenly and level the surface.

5 Make the sauce: Mix together the brown sugar and cocoa powder, then gradually blend in 1⅛ cups boiling water, stirring vigorously to avoid lumps. Pour the sauce over the mixture in the pie dish. The sauce cooks with the mixture in the oven. Do not worry if the mixture looks unpromising at this stage; during baking it rises above the sauce.

6 Bake just above the center of the oven for 40 minutes, or until the pudding is well risen and browned and the chocolate sauce beneath is syrupy.

7 Serve the pudding while it is hot, with ice cream or whipped cream, if liked.

VARIATION
For a special occasion, use dark rum instead of milk. Stir in 2 tablespoons chopped walnuts or blanched almonds at the end of stage 3.

CHOCOLATE TRIFLE

Preparation time: 8 minutes (roll); 10 minutes pudding
Cooling and chilling time: 30 minutes (roll)
1–1½ hours (trifle)
Finishing time: 10 minutes
Serves 6

1 package chocolate pudding
milk and sugar (see package)
1 12 oz can mandarin oranges
1½ cups heavy cream, whipped
chocolate sprinkles, to decorate

CHOCOLATE JELLY ROLL
½ cup all-purpose flour plus 2 tablespoons
2 tablespoons unsweetened cocoa
1 teaspoon baking powder
3 eggs
½ cup superfine sugar
strawberry jelly

1 Make the jelly roll: Preheat the oven to 375F. Grease a 13 × 9 inch jelly roll pan and line with lightly-oiled waxed paper.

2 Sift the flour, cocoa and baking powder together and set aside. In a large mixing bowl beat the eggs and sugar until thick and pale. Gradually fold in the dry ingredients, using a figure of eight movement, and spoon the batter into the prepared pan. Bake for 8–10 minutes.

3 Turn the cake out onto a clean dish towel liberally sprinkled with confectioners' sugar. Roll up the cake in the towel and let stand for at least 30 minutes or until quite cold. Unroll, spread the strawberry jelly and reroll.

4 Slice the jelly roll and use to line the base and sides of a glass serving bowl. Drain the oranges and sprinkle a little of the juice over the jellyroll slices. Arrange the oranges in the base of the bowl.

5 Make the pudding according to package directions, using sugar and milk, and pour the hot mixture into the prepared bowl. Cover the surface with plastic wrap to prevent the formation of a skin, and let stand until cool.

6 Refrigerate for at least 1 hour and then decorate the trifle with whipped cream and chocolate sprinkles.

ZUCCOTTO

Preparation time: 40 minutes
Chilling time: 12 hours
Finishing time: 20 minutes
Serves 6–8

½ cup hazelnuts, skinned
½ cup almonds, blanched
butter for greasing
¾ lb pound cake
2 tablespoons brandy
2 tablespoons Cointreau
2 tablespoons sweet cherry liqueur
5 oz unsweetened chocolate, into small pieces
2¼ cups heavy cream
¾ cup confectioner's sugar, sifted

DECORATION
sifted confectioner's sugar for sprinkling
1 tablespoon cocoa powder, sifted

1 Preheat the oven to 400F. Put the nuts onto 2 baking sheets and bake for 5 minutes.

2 Chop the hazelnuts with the almonds. Set aside.

3 Grease a 6 cup bowl thoroughly with butter, line it with plastic wrap, and generously butter the wrap.

4 Cut the cake into ½ inch slices. Moisten with the brandy and liqueurs and use to line the mold: arrange 3 slices in the bowl from the rim to the center, cutting them to a point where they fit together. Cut 3 more pieces slightly larger than the gaps, and press them tightly in place. Reserve the rest.

5 Melt 1 oz chocolate pieces (see page 9). Whip the cream until just stiff and fold in the sugar. Mix the nuts and 4 oz chocolate pieces into the cream. Spoon half the cream into the cake-lined mold, spreading it out in a thick layer.

6 Add the melted chocolate to the remaining cream and mix thoroughly. Spoon it into the mold and level the top.

7 Moisten the reserved cake with brandy and liqueurs. Cover the top of the mold with the smaller pieces of cake, filling any gaps. Cover with plastic wrap and weight with a plate. Refrigerate for at least 12 hours.

8 Up to 30 minutes before serving, invert a round serving dish over the mold and turn out the dessert. Remove the plastic wrap. Cut out a circle of waxed paper 10½ inches in diameter. Fold in half 3 times, to make eighths. Cut out each alternate section, without cutting through the center.

9 Sift confectioner's sugar all over the zuccotto. Mix 2 tablespoons confectioner's sugar with the cocoa. Place the paper pattern on top and sprinkle the cocoa in the cut-outs. Serve immediately.

MOCHA PANCAKES

Preparation time: 30 minutes
Cooking time: 25 minutes
Cooling time: 30 minutes
Finishing time: 5 minutes
Serves 12

- **1 cup plus 2 tablespoons all-purpose flour**
- **pinch of salt**
- **2 tablespoons sweetened cocoa powder**
- **2 tablespoons instant coffee**
- **2 tablespoons granulated sugar**
- **2 eggs, lightly beaten**
- **1 cup milk**
- **vegetable oil**
- **⅔ cup whipping cream, to decorate**
- **mandarin orange segments, drained, to decorate**

[1] Sift the flour, salt, cocoa powder and coffee into a bowl, then stir in the sugar. Make a well in the center. Add the eggs and 2 tablespoons of the milk and beat together, then slowly beat in enough milk to make a smooth batter the consistency of light cream. Strain the batter into a pitcher.

[2] Heat 1–2 teaspoons oil in a heavy based 6–7 inch frying pan over moderate to high heat. Pour off any excess oil.

[3] Beat the batter. Remove the frying pan from the heat and pour in about 2 tablespoons batter, tilting the pan to spread the batter evenly. Return to the heat, and cook for about 1 minute, or until the underside is set. Use the first pancake as a "tester" to judge the amount of batter needed and heat of pan.

[4] Turn the pancake over and cook for 30–60 seconds. Lift on to a sheet of waxed paper.

[5] Make 11 more pancakes, interleaving each with waxed paper. Stir batter frequently and grease the pan as necessary. Leave the pancakes to cool for about 30 minutes until just barely warm.

[6] Whip the cream until standing in soft peaks. Loosely roll up each pancake and arrange on a flat serving plate. Pipe or spoon a little cream on top of each pancake and arrange mandarin segments on top. Serve at once.

CHOCOLATE NUTTY TAPIOCA

Preparation time: 15 minutes
Cooking time: 45–60 minutes
Finishing time: 5–10 minutes
Serves 4

- 3 tablespoons tapioca
- 2 cups milk
- 2 tablespoons light soft brown sugar

TOPPING

- 2 tablespoons raw peanuts, skinned and coarsely chopped
- 1 oz semi-sweet chocolate, coarsely grated

1 Put the tapioca into a medium size heavy-based pan and pour in plenty of cold water. Bring to a boil, simmer for 5 minutes, then drain and return to the pan. The tapioca is cooked briefly in boiling water to soften it – otherwise the milk might evaporate before it has been absorbed.

2 Pour in the milk and bring slowly to a simmer. Cook, stirring frequently, for 45-60 minutes, until the tapioca is clear and the mixture is thick and creamy. Remove from the heat and stir in the sugar, to taste.

3 Preheat the broiler.

4 Turn the tapioca mixture into a shallow, flameproof dish. Level the surface, then sprinkle with the chopped peanuts and grated chocolate. Broil for 1–2 minutes, until the chocolate is melted and the nuts are lightly browned.

5 Serve hot or cold.

CHOCOLATE ORANGE MERINGUES

Preparation time: 30 minutes
Assembly time: 10 minutes
Serves 6

6 oz semi-sweet chocolate, broken into pieces
4 tablespoons orange-flavored liqueur, such as Cointreau, Triple Sec, Curacao or Grand Marnier
11 oz can mandarin orange segments, drained
6 meringue nests
⅔ cup whipping cream
2 tablespoons granulated sugar

[1] Put the chocolate into a bowl and add 2 tablespoons of the orange-flavored liqueur. Set the bowl over a pan of barely simmering water and leave until the chocolate has melted, stirring occasionally. Remove from the heat.

[2] Spear 12 orange segments with toothpicks. Pat them dry with paper towels, then dip them one at a time into the melted chocolate, to cover completely. Stick the coated oranges into 2 upturned grapefruit halves, so that they do not touch. Set aside for the chocolate to harden, about 15–20 minutes.

[3] Hold each meringue nest upside down, then dip it into the chocolate, leaving the base uncoated. Continue until all the meringues are coated on one side. Set the meringues aside on their bases for about 15 minutes, until the chocolate has hardened.

[4] When ready to assemble, divide the remaining orange segments into 6 heaps and arrange one heap on each meringue shell. Whip the cream until standing in stiff peaks, then fold in the remaining liqueur and the sugar. Spoon the cream over the orange segments or pipe it, using a piping bag fitted with a large star nozzle, to make a decorative border around each meringue nest.

[5] Remove the toothpicks from the chocolate-coated oranges and place 2 in the center of each of the meringue nests. Serve the chocolate orange meringues at once.

CHOCOLATE-CHERRY CHEESECAKE

Preparation time: 1¼ hours
Chilling time: overnight
Serves 8–10

15 oz can, pitted black cherries in heavy syrup
12 oz cream cheese
⅓ cup granulated sugar
2 eggs, separated
1 tablespoon Kirsch
1 tablespoon gelatine
1 cup whipping cream or a combination of whipping and heavy cream
4 oz semi-sweet chocolate, to decorate
1 tablespoon cornstarch
Kirsch or lemon juice, to taste

BASE
butter, for greasing
3 oz semi-sweet chocolate, broken
5 tablespoons butter
1¼ cups crumbled graham crackers

[1] First make the base: Line and grease the base of a 9 inch loose-bottomed round cake pan. In a small saucepan, melt the chocolate and butter over low heat, then mix in the graham cracker crumbs.

[2] Spread the mixture evenly over the base of the pan and press down well. Chill in the refrigerator while you make the filling.

[3] Drain the cherries, reserving the syrup. Cut them in half and spread one-third of them over the crumb base.

[4] In a large bowl, cream the cheese and sugar thoroughly. Beat in the yolks and Kirsch.

[5] Pour 2 tablespoons cold water into a small bowl and sprinkle in the gelatine. Leave for a few minutes to soften, then stand the bowl in very hot water and stir until the gelatine dissolves. Leave to cool slightly.

[6] Whip the cream until it just holds soft peaks. Beat the egg whites until they are stiff. Beat the gelatine slowly into the cheese mixture without letting lumps form. Fold in the cream, then the egg whites, using a metal spoon.

[7] Turn the mixture gently on to the chilled crumb base and spread evenly. Chill for several hours or overnight.

[8] Shortly before serving, decorate the cake. Shave long, thin curls of chocolate off the block (see page 9).

[9] Make a cherry sauce: Blend the cornstarch to a cream with a little of the reserved syrup. Pour the remaining syrup into a pan, adding Kirsch or lemon juice to taste. Bring slowly to a boil, then stir in the cornstarch mixture. Continue stirring until the liquid thickens and clears. Remove from the heat and cool under a piece of dampened waxed paper.

[10] Remove the cheesecake from the pan. Decorate with a ring of the remaining halved cherries. Spoon a little of the sauce over them. Arrange the chocolate around the edge of the cake and serve, with the rest of the sauce in a sauceboat.

HOT VANILLA CHOCOLATE SOUFFLE

Preparation time: 20 minutes
Standing time: 3 hours
Baking time: 40 minutes
Serves 4

margarine or butter, for greasing
2 tablespoons margarine or butter
2 tablespoons all-purpose flour
1 scant cup warm milk
2 tablespoons granulated sugar
3 egg yolks
1 teaspoon vanilla extract
4 egg whites
2 tablespoons chocolate chips
2 teaspoons confectioner's sugar, for dredging

1 Preheat the oven to 350F. Remove the top shelf so that it will not get in the way of the soufflé as it rises. Grease a 6 cup soufflé dish.

2 Melt the margarine or butter in a medium size, heavy-based saucepan. Sprinkle in the flour and stir over low heat for 1 minute. Remove from the heat and gradually stir in the milk. Return to low heat and simmer, stirring, until the mixture is thick and smooth.

3 Remove from the heat and stir in the sugar. Allow to cool slightly, then beat in the egg yolks, one at a time. Beat in the vanilla extract. Lay plastic wrap across the surface and leave the soufflé base to stand for 3 hours in a cool place.

4 Beat the egg whites until they stand in stiff peaks. Tip on to the vanilla mixture and fold in with a large metal spoon. When the egg whites are almost incorporated, fold in the chocolate chips.

5 Quickly turn the mixture into the prepared dish. Run a spatula through the mixture 1½ inches in from the edge. Bake just above the center of the oven for 40 minutes or until the soufflé is well risen and light golden in color. Do not open the oven door during cooking – the slightest draught can cause the soufflé to collapse.

6 Sift the confectioner's sugar over the top and serve at once.

CHOCOLATE MERINGUE LAYER

Preparation time: 30 minutes
Cooking time: 1½ hours
Finishing time: 1 hour
Serves 12-16

butter, for greasing
9 egg whites
pinch of salt
2¼ cups granulated sugar
6 cups heavy cream
8 oz semi-sweet chocolate, broken into pieces
chopped almonds, to decorate

1 Preheat the oven to 250F. Line 3 baking sheets with waxed paper and grease lightly with butter. Mark two circles 9–10 inches in diameter on 2 baking sheets.

2 Beat the egg whites and salt in a clean dry bowl until stiff and dry. Add half the sugar and beat well, then add the remaining sugar in 4 stages, beating well each time.

3 Spoon one-third of the mixture into a piping bag fitted with a large plain nozzle.

4 Pipe the meringue in a circle following the guideline on one baking sheet. Continue piping in decreasing circles inside the ring until the circle is filled. Refill the piping bag and repeat to form another round on the second baking sheet.

5 With the remaining third of the mixture, pipe 24 even-sized drops on to the third baking sheet.

6 Place the meringue rounds and the drops in the oven and leave until crisp and dry. The drops will take about 1 hour, and the rounds 1½ hours. Remove from the oven and leave to cool on a wire rack. Remove the paper when cool.

7 While the meringues are in the oven, beat the cream until thick enough to hold its shape. Melt the chocolate (see page 9).

8 When the small meringue drops are cool, dip the base of each one in the chocolate then set aside to allow the chocolate to harden.

9 Place one of the meringue rounds on a serving plate and spread with one-third of the cream. Position the other round on top.

10 Spread half the remaining cream over the top of the cake and trickle the remaining melted chocolate over the top. Swirl the chocolate lightly into the cream with a skewer, making circular movements to make an attractive design. Set aside in a cool place.

11 Fill a piping bag fitted with a star nozzle with the remaining cream and sandwich pairs of the meringue drops together with piped rosettes.

12 Sprinkle the chopped nuts over the center of the cake and pipe the remaining cream in rosettes around the top edge. Arrange the meringue drops around the cake and serve as soon as possible.

CHOCOLATE MOUSSE SPECIAL

Preparation time: 30 minutes
Chilling time: 2 hours
Finishing time: 5 minutes
Serves 4

4 oz semi-sweet chocolate, broken into pieces
few drops vanilla extract
3 eggs, separated
20–24 lady fingers
chocolate curls and orange slices, to decorate (optional)

1 Put the chocolate, vanilla extract and 1 tablespoon water into a heatproof bowl. Set the bowl over a pan half full of simmering water and leave, stirring occasionally, until the chocolate is melted. Set aside to cool slightly.

2 In a large bowl, beat the egg yolks until pale. Add the melted chocolate to the egg yolks and continue beating until the mixture is thick.

3 Beat the egg whites until standing in stiff peaks. Fold a spoonful of the egg whites into the chocolate mixture with a large metal spoon, then lightly fold in the rest.

4 Use half the lady fingers to line the base of an oblong 2 cup serving dish.

5 Pour the chocolate mixture over the cookies, then cover with plastic wrap. Refrigerate for at least 2 hours.

6 To serve: Arrange the remaining cookies, cut in half, on top of the mousse. Decorate with chocolate curls and orange slices, if liked, and serve chilled.

7 The mousse can be kept, covered, in the refrigerator for up to 48 hours.

CHOCOLATE MERINGUE PUDDING

Preparation time: 15 minutes
Baking time: 35 minutes
Finishing time: 10 minutes
Serves 4–6

butter, for greasing
1/4 cup butter or margarine
1/3 cup packed light brown sugar
1 tablespoon light corn syrup
1 egg, beaten
1 1/4 cups all-purpose flour
1/2 teaspoon baking powder
1/4 cup unsweetened cocoa
2/3 cup milk

CHOCOLATE SAUCE
1 tablespoon butter
4 oz semisweet chocolate
1 tablespoon milk

MERINGUE TOPPING
2 medium egg whites
1/4 cup superfine sugar
1 tablespoon granulated sugar

1 Preheat the oven to 350F. Grease a 5-cup ovenproof dish.

2 Beat the butter with the sugar until light and fluffy. Beat in the syrup and the egg.

3 Sift the flour and cocoa together and fold lightly into the creamed mixture with the milk.

4 Spoon the batter into the prepared dish and bake in the oven for 40–45 minutes.

5 Meanwhile, make the sauce: Put all the ingredients in a heatproof bowl over simmering water and beat until smooth.

6 Remove the cake from the oven and pour the sauce over the top. Increase the oven temperature to 425F.

7 For the topping, beat the egg whites until stiff. Fold in the superfine sugar lightly. Spread the meringue on top of the pudding, peaking it with the spoon. Sprinkle with granulated sugar.

8 Bake for 3–4 minutes until the meringue is just brown. Serve at once.

CHOCOLATE CHEESECAKE

Preparation time: 50 minutes
Chilling time: 3 hours
Serves 6–8

24 chocolate wafer cookies, finely crushed
⅔ cup butter, melted
mandarin orange segments to decorate

FILLING
1⅓ cups cottage cheese
8 oz cream cheese
¼ cup granulated sugar
juice of ½ lemon
¼ teaspoon vanilla extract
1¼ cup light cream
1 tablespoon powdered gelatine
3 oz plain semi-sweet chocolate, broken into pieces

1 Mix the crushed cookies with the butter. Press onto the base and sides of an oiled 8 inch loose-bottomed cake pan. Cover and chill for 30 minutes.

2 Meanwhile, make the filling: Press the cottage cheese through a strainer into a mixing bowl. Add the cream cheese and beat with a wooden spoon until well combined.

3 Add the sugar, lemon juice, vanilla and cream and mix well.

4 Sprinkle the gelatine over 3 tablespoons warm water in a bowl. Leave to soak for 2–3 minutes until spongy. Place the bowl over a saucepan of simmering water and stir until the gelatine has dissolved. Remove from the heat, leave to cool slightly, then stir gradually into the cheese mixture.

5 Melt the chocolate pieces (see page 9).

6 Pour the cheese mixture into the crust, then drizzle the melted chocolate over and swirl in with the point of a skewer. Take the skewer right down to the bottom to give a marbled effect right through.

7 Cover and chill for about 3 hours.

8 To serve: Run a knife around the edge of the cake, carefully remove the sides of the pan and slide the cheesecake onto a serving plate. Decorate with orange segments and serve chilled.

9 Store frozen for up to 1 month. To serve, unwrap and then defrost overnight in the refrigerator.

CHILLED CHOCOLATE SOUFFLE

Preparation time: 45–50 minutes
Chilling time: 2 hours
Serves 6

- 6 oz best quality semi-sweet chocolate
- 2 tablespoons strong black coffee
- 2 teaspoons powdered gelatine
- 4 eggs at room temperature, separated
- ⅓ cup granulated sugar
- 1 cup heavy cream
- generous pinch of salt
- confectioner's sugar or chocolate shavings (optional)

1 Break up the chocolate into a small, heatproof pitcher and pour the coffee over it. Dissolve the gelatine in ¼ cup water in a similar heatproof container and stand both containers in a saucepan of hot water over a very low heat.

2 Beat the egg yolks lightly in a large bowl and reserve.

3 Dissolve the sugar in ¼ cup water in a small, heavy-based saucepan. Boil over medium-high heat until the syrup reaches 240F on a sugar thermometer. Alternatively, check its readiness by dropping a little of the syrup into a saucer of cold water; it should form a soft ball.

4 Remove the saucepan from the heat immediately and pour the syrup into the egg yolks in a thin stream, beating continuously until the mixture is quite cool. When it is cool, remove the gelatine container from the water and beat in the tepid gelatine mixture.

5 Check that the pieces of chocolate are quite soft by prodding them with the tip of a sharp knife (if not, raise the heat briefly). Stir the chocolate until smooth, then beat it into the egg mixture.

6 Whip the cream until it holds peaks and stir it into the chocolate mixture.

7 Beat the egg whites with the salt until stiff. Carefully mix a little of the whites into the chocolate mixture, then fold in the rest, using the cutting edge of a metal spoon.

8 Tie a strip of waxed paper or foil around the outside of a 3½ cup soufflé dish so that it sticks up about 1 inch above the rim. Pour the mixture into it and refrigerate for at least 2 hours, until the soufflé is firm.

9 Remove the waxed paper and, if wished, lightly sprinkle the top with confectioner's sugar. Alternatively, carefully press chocolate shavings around the edge before serving, to make a decorative border.

CHOCOLATE AND HAZELNUT MOUSSE

Preparation time: 20 minutes
Chilling time: 2 hours
Finishing time: 30 minutes
Serves 4

4 oz semi-sweet chocolate, broken into pieces
2 tablespoons butter
3 eggs, separated
2 teaspoons Cointreau (optional)
butter cookies, to serve (optional)

DECORATION
2 tablespoons hazelnuts
4 tablespoons heavy cream

1 Put the chocolate pieces in a bowl with the butter. Place over a pan of barely simmering water and heat gently until melted. Stir gently.

2 Remove from the heat and pour into a large bowl. Cool slightly.

3 Beat the egg yolks together, then beat into the chocolate. Stir in the Cointreau, if using.

4 In a clean dry bowl, beat the egg whites until they form soft peaks, then gently fold into the chocolate mixture.

5 Spoon the mixture into 4 stemmed wine or dessert glasses, smooth the surface and refrigerate for at least 2 hours.

6 Meanwhile, skin the hazelnuts. Preheat the oven to 350F. Roast the nuts for 15–20 minutes, then rub off the skins with a cloth. Leave to cool, then chop the nuts finely.

7 Just before serving, lightly whip the cream and pipe a rosette on the top of each mousse. Decorate with chopped hazelnuts. Serve with butter cookies, if liked.

CHOCOLATE NUT PUDDINGS

Preparation time: 30 minutes
Cooking time: 40–45 minutes
Serves 8

butter for greasing
1 stick butter, softened
¼ cup granulated sugar
⅓ cup finely chopped hazelnuts
½ cup crushed graham crackers
4 oz semi-sweet chocolate, grated
4 eggs, separated
4 teaspoons brandy

CHOCOLATE SAUCE
⅓ cup superfine sugar
juice and grated rind of 1 large orange
8 oz semi-sweet chocolate

1 Preheat the oven to 400F.

2 Cut 8 discs of waxed paper to fit the bases of eight ½ cup molds. Lightly butter the bases of the molds and fit in the discs of waxed paper. Lightly butter the molds and the paper.

3 Cream the butter, add the sugar gradually and beat until the mixture is light and fluffy. Stir in the hazelnuts, graham cracker crumbs and grated chocolate. Beat in the egg yolks one at a time. Add the brandy.

4 In a clean bowl, beat the egg whites to stiff peaks. With a large metal spoon, carefully fold the egg whites into the nut mixture.

5 Spoon the pudding into the prepared molds, filling them three-quarters full. Cover each mould with a disc of foil, twisting it tightly under the rim to seal.

6 Stand the molds in a roasting pan and pour in enough hot water to come halfway up the sides of the molds. Cook in the oven for 40–45 minutes or until a skewer inserted in the center of a pudding comes out clean.

7 Meanwhile, in a saucepan, bring ½ cup water, the sugar, orange juice and grated orange rind to a boil and simmer for 3 minutes. Remove from the heat.

8 Melt the chocolate (see page 9) and pour it into the syrup in a steady stream, beating to a smooth consistency.

9 Run a sharp knife around the edge of each mold and turn the puddings onto a heated serving platter or into individual bowls. Pour the chocolate sauce over each one and serve immediately.

BUTTER CREAM CASSATA

Preparation time: 45 minutes
Chilling time: 3 hours
Finishing time: 10 minutes
Serves 6–8

1/3 cup granulated sugar
1 stick sweet butter
2 egg yolks
1 oz semi-sweet chocolate, broken into pieces
2 tablespoons hazelnuts, lightly toasted, skins rubbed off and chopped
3 tablespoons cocoa powder, sifted
9 oz pound cake, cut into very thin, even slices
6 tablespoons rum

PRALINE
vegetable oil for greasing
2 tablespoons granulated sugar
1 teaspoon lemon juice
2 tablespoons almonds, blanched and peeled

DECORATION
3/4 cup whipped cream
grated chocolate
almonds or hazelnuts

1 Make the praline: Lightly oil a cold baking sheet lined with foil. Melt the sugar in 1½ teaspoons water and the lemon juice in a heavy pan over very low heat. When the sugar has dissolved, boil the syrup over medium heat until golden. Remove from the heat and stir in the almonds thoroughly. Pour onto the oiled surface and leave to harden. When set, carefully peel off the foil. Put the praline between sheets of waxed paper and crush with a rolling pin.

2 Butter a rectangular 3½ cup loaf pan and line it with foil. Butter the foil. Cream the sugar and butter until light and fluffy. Add the egg yolks, one at a time, beating thoroughly. Divide the mixture between 3 bowls. Add the praline to the first, the hazelnuts and chocolate to the second and the cocoa to the third.

3 Brush the cake slices with the rum. Cover the bottom of the pan evenly with one-quarter of the slices in a layer and spread with praline cream. Cover with a second layer of cake and spread with chocolate and hazelnut cream. Cover with a third layer of cake, and spread with cocoa cream. End with a layer of cake. Cover with foil and chill.

4 When well chilled, turn out onto a chilled dish, cover with the whipped cream and decorate with grated chocolate and almonds or hazelnuts.

CHOCOLATE PINEAPPLE RINGS

Preparation time: 45 minutes
Baking time: 20 minutes
Finishing time: 20 minutes
Makes 10

- ⅔ cup butter
- ¼ cup granulated sugar
- 1½ cups all-purpose flour
- 3 tablespoons ground almonds
- ¼ teaspoon almond extract
- 8 oz semi-sweet chocolate
- 10 canned pineapple rings
- 10 stemmed maraschino cherries
- 1 teaspoon cornstarch

1 Preheat the oven to 375F. Line a baking sheet with non-stick paper.

2 In a mixing bowl, cream 8 tablespoons of the butter and all of the granulated sugar together with a wooden spoon until the mixture is light and fluffy.

3 Add the flour, ground almonds and almond extract and knead the mixture with your hands until it forms a soft dough.

4 Lightly flour a wooden board. Turn the dough out onto the board and roll it out thinly. With a 3 inch round pastry cutter, cut out about 20 rounds. Place the rounds on the lined baking sheet.

5 Prick the surface of each round with a fork and bake them in the oven for about 20 minutes, or until they are lightly brown. Transfer to a wire rack to cool.

6 In a small saucepan, melt the chocolate and the remaining butter over very low heat, stirring constantly with a wooden spoon until the mixture is smooth and thick. Add 1–2 tablespoons lukewarm water to the mixture to thin it slightly if necessary.

7 Spread the chocolate mixture generously over each cookie. Sandwich 2 cookie rounds together while the chocolate is still soft.

8 Drain the pineapple rings, reserving 4 tablespoons of the can liquid, and place one ring on each of the cookie sandwiches before the chocolate has set. Put a cherry in the middle of each pineapple ring. Set aside.

9 In a small saucepan, mix the cornstarch with the reserved pineapple juice. Over moderately high heat, bring the syrup to the boil, stirring constantly. Cook until it has thickened.

10 Remove the pan from the heat and allow the syrup to cool to room temperature. With a pastry brush spread the syrup over the pineapple rings. Let the syrup glaze set for 10 minutes before serving.

CHOCOLATE PUDDING

Preparation time: 20 minutes
Baking time: 30–40 minutes
Serves 6

- 1 stick butter
- 1½ cups all-purpose flour
- ½ teaspoon salt
- 1 teaspoon baking powder
- ½ cup granulated sugar
- ¼ cup cocoa powder
- 2 eggs, lightly beaten
- 5 tablespoons milk
- ¼ teaspoon vanilla extract

1 Preheat the oven to 375F.

2 Using 1 tablespoon of the butter, grease a medium size pie or soufflé dish.

3 Sift the flour, salt and baking powder into a medium size mixing bowl. With your fingertips, rub the remaining butter into the mixture. Stir in the sugar and cocoa.

4 With a wooden spoon, beat in the eggs and milk until the mixture is smooth and of a dropping consistency. Add the vanilla extract and mix thoroughly.

5 Pour the mixture into the dish and bake just above the center of the oven for 30–40 minutes, or until a skewer inserted into the pudding comes out clean.

6 Remove the pudding from the oven and serve from the dish, with chocolate sauce (see page 14).

Ice creams and Iced Desserts

Making ice cream is by no means a complicated and difficult task, requiring expensive equipment – as these easy recipes show. So, why not make your own melt-in-the-mouth ices or turn plain supermarket ice cream into the *pièce de résistance* for a party? From Iced Chocolate Truffles Truffles to Flambéed Iced Cream Pudding, these refreshing ideas cannot fail to please.

ICED CHOCOLATE TRUFFLES

Preparation time: 50 minutes
Freezing time: overnight
Serves 6

½ cup maraschino cherries
¼ cup cherry liqueur
16 oz dark chocolate, grated
1 quart chocolate ice cream
1¼ cups heavy cream
¼ teaspoon vanilla extract
6 maraschino cherries, to decorate

1 Cut the cherries into quarters. Mix the chopped cherries and liqueur and chill overnight. Place the chocolate in an airtight container.

2 The day before serving, soften the ice cream in the refrigerator for 15–20 minutes. Make 6 balls with a large ice cream scoop. Press 1 tablespoon drained cherries into the center of each. Smooth over and freeze for 10 minutes or until very firm. Roll each ball in grated chocolate until evenly coated and return to the freezer.

3 Whip the cream with the vanilla until stiff. Pipe a small swirl on to 6 chilled dessert plates; place 1 truffle on each swirl. Return to the freezer until ready to serve.

ICE CREAM STRIPE

Preparation time: 1½ hours
Freezing time: 3–4 hours
Serves 6

1¼ pints chocolate ice cream
1¼ pints vanilla ice cream
1¼ pints coffee ice cream
oil for greasing
whipped cream and chopped nuts to decorate

PRALINE
½ cup granulated sugar
⅓ cup almonds, unpeeled

1 Put the ice cream in the main part of the refrigerator to soften. Chill a 7 cup loaf pan and grease a baking sheet.

2 Make the praline: Put the sugar and nuts in a heavy-based saucepan and melt the sugar over a very low heat. Do not stir.

3 Once the sugar has dissolved, turn the heat up a little and stir the nuts into the caramel. Cook carefully until the syrup turns a deep golden color. Turn the praline out onto the baking sheet and leave to harden.

4 Once the praline has set, remove it from the baking sheet and crush it to a fine powder.

5 Remove the chocolate ice cream from the refrigerator and spoon it into the loaf pan, level it off and sprinkle with half the praline. Put in the freezer for a few minutes to firm up a little. Repeat with the vanilla ice cream and the remaining praline. Again put in the freezer for a few minutes to firm. Spoon the coffee ice cream on top and smooth. Freeze for at least 3–4 hours to harden.

6 To serve: Unmold the ice cream about 15 minutes before serving and leave in the refrigerator to soften slightly. Serve whole, decorated with whipped cream and chopped nuts, or in decorated slices.

CHOCOLATE ICE CREAM BALLS

Preparation time: 30 minutes
Freezing time: 3–4 hours
Makes 30 balls

300 ml/½ pint vanilla ice-cream
grated zest of 1 orange
few drops of orange liqueur flavouring
150 g/5 oz plain chocolate cake covering

1 Let the ice-cream soften slightly, then beat in the grated orange zest and the flavouring. Do not use real liqueur as it will inhibit freezing and the balls will not go hard; choose instead a concentrated essence or flavouring of any liqueur.

2 Using a melon baller, scoop the hard ice-cream into tiny balls. Put these on the cold baking sheet and push cocktail sticks into each one. Freeze for several hours until hard.

3 Melt the chocolate cake covering (see page 9) and pour it into a tall glass.

4 Working quickly, dip the ice-cream balls into the chocolate, then put them back on the baking sheet. Return to the freezer until you are ready to serve them.

CHOCOLATE ORANGE SUNDAE

Preparation time: 30 minutes
Cooling time: 1 hour
Freezing time: 4–5 hours
Finishing time: 20 minutes
Serves 6

7 oz semi-sweet chocolate, broken into pieces
1¼ cups milk
2 tablespoons cocoa powder
1 egg
1 egg yolk
¼ cup granulated sugar
1¼ cups heavy cream
2–4 tablespoons orange-flavored liqueur

TOPPING
¾ cup heavy cream
1 teaspoon granulated sugar
1 tablespoon orange-flavored liqueur
whole, fresh strawberries and orange slices, to decorate

1 Put the chocolate into a pan with the milk and cocoa powder. Heat gently until the chocolate melts. Remove the pan from the heat and stir the chocolate milk until smooth.

2 Beat the egg and the yolk with the sugar until pale. Pour on the chocolate milk, stirring all the time. Strain and allow to cool for 1 hour.

3 Whip the cream until it just holds its shape. Fold it carefully into the chocolate mixture, alternately with the orange liqueur. Pour the mixture into a freezerproof container and freeze for about 3 hours, until almost firm.

4 Beat vigorously to break down the ice crystals and return to the freezer for an hour. If possible, beat a second time for a really smooth result. Cover and freeze for a further hour or until required.

5 Make the topping: Whip the cream with the sugar and orange-flavored liqueur until stiff.

6 About 10 minutes before serving, remove the ice cream from the freezer to soften slightly. Just before serving, spoon it into tall sundae glasses, top with the orange-flavored cream and decorate with a slice of orange and a whole strawberry. Serve at once.

FLAMBEED ICED CREAM PUDDING

Soaking time: 2 hours
Preparation time: 30 minutes
Freezing time: 4½–5½ hours
Serves 8

¼ cup maraschino cherries
¼ cup dried apricots
¼ cup pitted dates
4 tablespoons seedless raisins
2 tablespoons candied peel
6 tablespoons brandy
1¾ cups heavy cream
¾ cup confectioner's sugar, sifted
1 teaspoon vanilla extract

CHOCOLATE COATING
6 oz semi-sweet chocolate, broken into pieces
2 tablespoons butter

1 Cut the cherries, apricots and dates into small pieces, then put them in a bowl with the raisins and peel.

2 Add half the brandy to the fruit and mix well. Cover and leave to stand for at least 2 hours, stirring occasionally, until the fruit has softened and absorbed all the alcohol.

3 Pour the cream into a bowl, add the confectioner's sugar and vanilla and beat until it forms soft peaks. Fold in the soaked fruit.

4 Spoon the cream mixture into a 3½ cup soufflé dish and smooth the top. Cover with plastic wrap and freeze for 4–5 hours until frozen solid.

5 Remove from the freezer, then dip a palette knife in hot water and run it around the edge. Place a round of foil on top of the pudding, turn out onto a wire rack and return it to the freezer while you are preparing the chocolate coating.

6 Put the chocolate, butter and 2 tablespoons of water in a bowl. Set the bowl over a pan half full of simmering water and leave, stirring occasionally, until the chocolate has melted.

7 Remove the pudding from the freezer and place the rack over a plate. Pour the chocolate coating over the frozen pudding, smoothing it around the sides with a palette knife to coat completely – the chocolate does not have to be completely smooth. Return to the freezer until the chocolate hardens.

8 Pour the remaining brandy into a pan and heat gently.

9 To serve: Remove the pudding from the freezer, peel off the foil around the base and place the pudding on a serving plate. Light the warmed brandy and pour, flaming, over the pudding. Allow to flame until the chocolate starts to bubble around the base, then blow out the flames and serve.

10 To store: Prepare to the end of stage 7. Wrap in plastic wrap and foil. The pudding can then be frozen for up to 3 months.

ICED CHOCOLATE BOXES

Preparation time: 15 minutes
Serves 6

1 pint block of chocolate ice cream
24 wafer-thin peppermint chocolates
¾ cup heavy cream
11 oz can mandarin orange segments, drained
6 small sprigs fresh mint, to decorate (optional)

1 Cut the ice cream into 6 equal cubes and place the cubes on a freezer-proof plate. (Note: Soft scoop ice cream is *not* suitable for this recipe, as it does not hold its shape sufficiently well.) Press 1 peppermint chocolate wafer onto 4 sides of each cube, leaving the top and bottom plain. Return the cubes to the freezer, or freezing compartment of the refrigerator, while you prepare the cream for the topping.

2 Whip the cream until thick, but not stiff, then put into a piping bag fitted with a large star nozzle.

3 Remove the chocolate boxes from the freezer and pipe the cream in a decorative whirl on the top of each box. Top with orange segments and a sprig of mint, if liked. Place on chilled, individual serving plates and serve immediately, before the ice cream melts.

4 To store: Prepare the boxes up to the end of stage 1; open freeze the cubes, then place them in a single layer in a rigid container. Cover and return to the freezer for up to 1 month. Use the iced chocolate boxes straight from the freezer; decorate with cream, orange segments and mint and serve.

CHOCOLATE ICE CREAM

Preparation time: 20 minutes
Cooling time: 30 minutes
Freezing time: 3–5 hours
Finishing time: 30 minutes
Serves 6

½ cup granulated sugar
2½ cups whipping cream
4 oz semi-sweet chocolate, chopped
5 egg yolks
2 oz semi-sweet chocolate caraque (see page 10)

1 If using the freezing compartment of your refrigerator, turn it down to its lowest temperature (the highest setting) about an hour before you start.

2 Put the sugar, cream and chopped chocolate in the top of a double boiler and bring to a boil over simmering water, stirring occasionally, until the chocolate melts.

3 In a bowl, beat the egg yolks together lightly. Pour the chocolate cream mixture over the egg yolks, beating constantly.

4 Return the cream to the double boiler and heat until just simmering. Do not let it boil.

5 Strain the chocolate cream into a shallow, freezerproof container and stand over ice until cooled.

6 Cover and freeze for about 1 hour, or until the mixture hardens to a depth of 1 inch around the sides of the container. Remove from the freezer and beat vigorously with a fork or wire whisk to break up the ice crystals. Spoon the mixture into an 8½ inch cake pan and level the surface. Cover with foil and freeze again until firm.

7 About 30 minutes before serving, transfer the ice cream to the main part of the refrigerator to soften slightly.

8 Ease the ice cream away from the sides of the pan with a palette knife and invert the pan onto a flat serving plate. Cover the pan briefly with a cloth wrung out in hot water and lift it off. Decorate with semi-sweet chocolate caraque.

Illustrated on page 67.

MINT AND CHOCOLATE ICE CREAM

Preparation time: 40 minutes
Freezing time: 3–5 hours
Finishing time: 30 minutes
Serves 6

¼ cup granulated sugar
3 egg yolks
¾ cup light cream
¾ cup heavy cream
5–6 tablespoons crème de menthe
4 oz semi-sweet chocolate, coarsely chopped

1 If using the freezing compartment of your refrigerator, turn it down to its lowest temperature (the highest setting) about an hour before you start.

2 Put the sugar in a saucepan with ½ cup water and stir over a gentle heat until dissolved. Then boil until the syrup reaches a temperature of 101C/215F on a sugar thermometer or until it forms a thread when pulled between 2 spoons.

3 Beat the egg yolks together lightly in a bowl. Pour the syrup onto the egg yolks in a thin stream, beating constantly until the yolks become pale yellow.

4 In another bowl, whip the creams together until soft peaks form. Fold in the beaten egg yolks, crème de menthe and coarsely chopped chocolate.

5 Pour the ice cream mixture into a shallow, freezerproof container, cover and freeze for about 1 hour.

6 Beat vigorously with a fork or wire whisk to break down the ice crystals. Spoon it into a chilled 3½ cup jello mold, press it in firmly, then cover and freeze again until firmly frozen.

7 About 30 minutes before serving, transfer it to the refrigerator to soften slightly. Invert the mold over a flat serving plate and cover it with a cloth wrung out in hot water. Leave for just a second or two, then very carefully remove the mold.

CONFECTIONERY AND PETITS FOURS

Boxed Rum Truffles make a most attractive (and delicious!) present, ideal for family and friends alike – and confections like Pineapple and Date Delights are reminders of how candy used to taste. For the perfect end to a dinner party, try serving delicate petits fours – like Chocolate-dipped Candied Peel or Cigarettes Russes – with the after-dinner coffee.

MERINGUE PETITS FOURS

Preparation time: 40 minutes
Baking time: 1¼ hours
Cooling time: 40–50 minutes
Finishing time: 20 minutes
Makes 40

melted butter and sifted flour for baking sheets
2 egg whites
pinch of salt
½ cup granulated sugar
3 oz semi-sweet chocolate, broken into pieces
¾ cup heavy cream
grated rind of ½ orange
2–3 teaspoons orange-flavored liqueur

1 Preheat the oven to 150F.

2 Brush 2 baking sheets with melted butter and sprinkle evenly with sifted flour.

3 Place the egg whites and a pinch of salt in a large bowl. Beat with an electric beater, starting slowly and increasing speed as they begin to foam, until stiff but not dry.

4 Continue beating and add 2 tablespoons of the sugar, 1 tablespoon at a time. Change to a large wire whisk and beat until smooth and glossy. With a large metal spoon, fold in the remaining sugar.

5 Fit a piping bag with a ¼ inch plain nozzle and spoon in the meringue mixture. Pipe 80 small shells on the prepared baking sheets.

6 Bake for 1¼ hours until crisp but still white on the outside and slightly softer inside. Remove from the oven. With a palette knife, transfer the meringues to a wire rack and leave them for 1 hour to cool completely.

7 Melt the chocolate (see page 9). Dip 40 of the meringue shells in the melted chocolate and set aside to harden. They should be thickly coated, so that the meringue is completely masked by the chocolate.

8 Store in an airtight container until ready to use.

9 Make the filling: Whip the thick cream until stiff and fold in the grated orange rind and liqueur. Sandwich a little of the flavored cream between a white shell and a chocolate-covered shell and repeat to make 40 petits fours. Chill and serve within 2–3 hours.

PINEAPPLE AND DATE DELIGHTS

Preparation time: 1¼–1½ hours
Setting time: 1½ hours
Makes 40

2 oz semi-sweet chocolate, broken into pieces
4 rings fresh or drained canned pineapple
2 tablespoons unsalted pistachio nuts, finely chopped
3 oz semi-sweet chocolate broken into pieces
1 tablespoon orange-flavored liqueur
thinly pared rind of 1 large orange, finely shredded
16 whole skinned and pitted fresh dates, or pitted dried dates

[1] Melt 2 oz of the chocolate (see page 9).

[2] Meanwhile, cut each pineapple ring into 6 equal pieces and dry the pieces thoroughly. Place the chopped nuts on a small plate.

[3] Remove the bowl of melted chocolate from the pan. Holding a piece of pineapple between your fingers, dip the rounded end in the chocolate, then in the nuts. Place on waxed paper. Dip the remaining pineapple in the same way and leave on the waxed paper to set. If the kitchen is very warm, transfer the pineapple, on the paper, to a cool place (but not the refrigerator) to speed up setting.

[4] Bring a saucepan of water to a boil. Add the strips of orange rind, bring back to a boil and simmer for 1 minute. Drain the strips thoroughly, then dry on paper towels and set aside.

[5] Melt the rest of the chocolate with the orange-flavored liqueur (see page 9).

[6] Remove the bowl of melted chocolate from the pan. Spear a date on a skewer, then coat in the chocolate.

[7] Using a fork, ease the date off the skewer onto waxed paper and decorate with a few strips of orange rind. Coat and decorate the remaining dates in the same way and leave to set. Make sure that the covered dates do not touch each other.

[8] To serve: carefully remove from the waxed paper and place in small paper cases.

CIGARETTES RUSSES

Preparation time: 1¼ hours
Makes 15–20

butter and flour for greasing
2 egg whites
¾ cup confectioner's sugar, sifted
5 tablespoons all-purpose flour
5 tablespoons butter, melted
few drops of vanilla extract
1 oz semi-sweet chocolate

1 Preheat the oven to 400F. Lightly grease 2 baking sheets with butter and dust them with flour.

2 In a bowl, beat the egg whites until stiff. Sift the confectioner's sugar onto them and gently beat it in with a wooden spoon. Be careful not to knock the air out of the egg whites.

3 Sift the flour on to the mixture. Beat it in carefully, making sure that the mixture is well combined. Then beat in the melted butter and vanilla.

4 Drop 1 tablespoon of the mixture on to 1 of the prepared baking sheets. Smooth the mixture out thinly and evenly with a knife. Bake for 5–6 minutes until the cookie is set and golden brown. Repeat with another tablespoonful of the mixture on the other baking sheet, halfway through the cooking of the first cookie.

5 Run a palette knife or spatula under one baked cookie and turn it upside down. Quickly roll it up around the handle of a wooden spoon. After a few seconds, when each biscuit has hardened, remove the wooden spoon and cool the rolled cookie on a wire tray.

6 Cook the remaining mixture in staggered batches, in the same way. It is important to cook these elegant cookies one at a time, to ensure that they are soft for rolling.

7 Melt the chocolate (see page 9). Dip one end of each cookie into the molten chocolate. Use the end of a wooden spoon to clear the chocolate from the center of the cookies. Put the cookies back on the wire tray until the chocolate has cooled and hardened.

8 Cigarettes russes can be stored for up to 2 weeks in an airtight container. They must be kept in a cool place.

CHOCOLATE CASES

Preparation time: 35 minutes
Setting time: 8 hours
Assembly time: 10–15 minutes
Makes 18–20

7 oz good quality, semi-sweet baking chocolate, broken into pieces
1 tablespoon coffee and chicory extract
4 tablespoons butter, softened
2 tablespoons dark rum
"leaves" of angelica and colored dragees, to decorate

1 Make the chocolate cases: Melt 4 oz chocolate (see page 9). Remove the bowl from the pan.

2 Put 1 heaped teaspoon melted chocolate into a paper petits fours case. Press in another, gently forcing the chocolate up between the cases. Prepare 18–20 chocolate cases and stand them on a large flat plate.

3 Make the filling: Melt the remaining chocolate as in stage 1. Remove the bowl from the pan and beat in the flavoring. Add the butter, a little at a time, and continue beating until the mixture is smooth and glossy. Stir in the rum. Cover the bowl with plastic wrap. Leave the cases and filling at room temperature for 8 hours, or overnight, to firm.

4 Assemble the cases: Very gently peel the inner and then the outer paper cases away from the chocolate cases. Stand the chocolate cases on a cool, flat surface.

5 Put the filling in a piping bag fitted with a small star nozzle and pipe a swirl into each case. Decorate with a "leaf" of angelica and a colored dragee. Serve the chocolate cases as soon as possible, from a chilled serving plate.

RUM TRUFFLES

Preparation time: 45–60 minutes
Chilling time: 1½ hours
Makes 18

- **8 oz semi-sweet chocolate, broken into pieces**
- **2 tablespoons cold, unsweetened strong black coffee**
- **3 tablespoons heavy cream**
- **2 tablespoons dark rum or brandy**
- **2 tablespoons cocoa powder for coating**

[1] Put the chocolate into a large bowl. Add the coffee and cream. Set the bowl over a pan of barely simmering water and leave until the chocolate has melted, stirring the mixture occasionally.

[2] Remove the bowl from the pan. Beat the chocolate mixture for 10–15 minutes, until thick enough to stand in soft peaks. Add the rum or brandy and beat for a further 2–3 minutes to mix well.

[3] Using a rubber spatula, scrape the mixture into a small bowl. Cover and refrigerate for about 1½ hours, or until firm but not solid. If the mixture is very stiff, work it with a wooden spoon until just softened. Chill a baking sheet.

[4] Sift the cocoa over the chilled baking sheet.

[5] Drop heaped teaspoonfuls of the chocolate mixture onto the cocoa. Lightly coat your fingertips, by pressing them into the cocoa. Shape each heap into a ball between your fingertips, then roll in the cocoa until evenly coated.

[6] Continue making truffles until all the mixture is used. Chill for 5 minutes to firm. Serve at room temperature.

[7] Truffles will keep for 2–3 days in a covered plastic container in the refrigerator.

MARZIPAN TRUFFLES

Preparation time: 45–60 minutes
Chilling time: 1 hour
Makes 30

- **vegetable oil for greasing**
- **¼ cup shelled almonds**
- **¼ cup granulated sugar**
- **6 oz semi-sweet chocolate, broken into pieces**
- **3 tablespoons butter**
- **2 tablespoons light corn syrup**
- **3 tablespoons brandy or rum**
- **¾ cup cake crumbs**
- **confectioner's sugar, for dusting**
- **1 lb marzipan**
- **4 tablespoons granulated sugar, for coating**
- **angelica sticks, to decorate**

[1] Grease a baking sheet with oil. Put the almonds and sugar in a small heavy-based pan and heat gently, stirring, until the sugar has dissolved. Bring to a boil and boil until the syrup turns deep golden. Then plunge the pan base into ice water.

[2] Leave the pan in the water until the sizzling stops, then pour the syrup into the prepared baking tray. When cold, crush finely.

[3] Put the chocolate, butter, syrup and brandy in a bowl over a pan of barely simmering water. Leave until the chocolate and butter have melted, stirring occasionally.

[4] Remove the bowl from the pan. Stir in the almond mixture and the cake crumbs. Mix well, then cover and chill for 30 minutes until firm, but not solid.

[5] Line a baking sheet with non-stick parchment. Form teaspoonfuls of the chocolate mixture into balls and place on the prepared tray. Chill for 30 minutes until solid.

[6] Dust a working surface with confectioner's sugar and roll out the marzipan to a rectangle measuring 24×20 inches. Cut out 30 circles with a diameter of 2½ inches.

[7] With damp hands, wrap each chocolate ball in a circle of marzipan, molding it between your palms until smooth, then roll in the sugar to coat. Push angelica sticks into each ball. Serve at room temperature.

[8] Truffles will keep for 1-2 weeks in a covered plastic container in the refrigerator.

CHOCOLATE CREAM MINTS

Preparation time: 20 minutes
Chilling time: 4 hours
Finishing time: 5 minutes
Makes 64 mints

14 oz semi-sweet dessert chocolate, broken into pieces
2 tablespoons butter
¾ cup heavy cream
1 tablespoon peppermint extract

1 Put the chocolate, butter and cream into a bowl over a pan of simmering water. Heat gently until the chocolate has melted, then remove from the heat and stir until smooth. Stir in the peppermint extract and allow to cool for 5 minutes.

2 Meanwhile, line an 8 inch shallow, square cake pan with foil or waxed paper.

3 Beat the chocolate mixture until it is smooth and glossy. Pour it into the prepared pan and level the top. Chill for 4 hours, until set.

4 Loosen the chocolate-mint mixture from the sides of the pan and lift it out on the paper, on to a wooden board.

5 Cut it into neat fingers, using a sharp knife. Serve at once or chill until required.

6 The chocolate mints will keep for 3–4 days in the refrigerator.

CHOCOLATE KIRSCH TWIRLS

Preparation time: 30 minutes
Setting time: overnight
Makes about 18

8 oz semi-sweet chocolate
3 tablespoons very strong black coffee
4 tablespoons butter, softened
2 egg yolks
1 tablespoon Kirsch
18 black cherries, fresh or canned, pitted

[1] Melt half the chocolate (see page 9).

[2] Spoon about 1 teaspoon melted chocolate into a small paper case. Put another case on top and press the cases together to squeeze the chocolate up the sides. Repeat with the remaining chocolate. Place the cases on a baking sheet and refrigerate overnight.

[3] Melt the remaining chocolate in the same way, then stir in the coffee. Remove from the heat and leave to cool slightly.

[4] Meanwhile take the chocolate cases out of the refrigerator and peel off the paper, keeping your hands cool by washing them in cold water when necessary. Put the chocolate cases back into the refrigerator to firm.

[5] Beat the softened butter into the chocolate-coffee mixture, then stir in the egg yolks and Kirsch.

[6] If you are using canned cherries, drain them well and dry on paper towels. If fresh, pit and wash them. Put one cherry into each case.

[7] Spoon the chocolate-Kirsch mixture into a piping bag fitted with a ½ inch star nozzle. Pipe some of the mixture into each case to cover the cherries.

[8] Put the twirls into fresh paper cases and chill until you are ready to serve them.

CHOCOLATE-DIPPED CANDIED PEEL

Preparation time: 30 minutes
Drying time: 2 days
Finishing time: 15 minutes
Makes about 30

1 large orange
1 large lemon
½ cup granulated sugar
¼ cup superfine sugar
1 oz semi-sweet chocolate

[1] Scrub the orange and lemon and cut into quarters. Scrape away the flesh, reserving it for another recipe. Cut the peel into long narrow strips.

[2] Put the peel strips in a saucepan and cover with cold water. Bring to a boil, then drain. Return to the saucepan and cover with cold water again. Bring to a boil, then simmer over gentle heat for about 1½-2 hours, until the peel is soft, but not mushy. Add more water if necessary.

[3] Leave the peel to cool completely in the liquid, then drain.

[4] Put the granulated sugar and ¼ cup water in a pan and stir over a gentle heat until the sugar has dissolved. Add the peel and simmer until the peel has absorbed all the syrup.

[5] Turn the peel onto a wire rack covered with waxed paper. Using tongs, separate the pieces of peel so they do not touch each other. Put the trays in a warm place for 2 days until the peel feels almost dry.

[6] Sift the superfine sugar onto a plate and roll each piece of peel in the sugar. Store in an airtight container for up to 6 months.

[7] To finish, melt the chocolate (see page 9). Dip one end of each piece of peel into the chocolate. Set out to dry on non-stick paper. The peel will keep for 1–2 weeks in an airtight container kept in a cool and dry place.

KIDS' TREATS

Most children love chocolate and once in a while it does no harm to indulge them – after all, a little of what you fancy does you good! If time is precious, simply whip up a batch of Chocolate Banana Pops or Chocolate Walnut Fudge. For a special occasion, a little time and effort will produce a centerpiece to remember – our Spaceship Cake is sure to be a winner.

YUMMY CHOCOLATE CAKE

Preparation time: 15 minutes
Baking time: 20–25 minutes
Cooling time: 2 hours
Finishing time: 65–80 minutes
Serves 8–10

2 cups all-purpose flour
1 teaspoon baking powder
2 tablespoons cocoa powder
pinch of salt
1 cup granulated sugar
2 large eggs
5 tablespoons condensed milk
1 teaspoon vanilla flavouring
⅓ cup margarine, melted

FILLING AND TOPPING
1⅔ cups confectioner's sugar
3 tablespoons sweetened cocoa powder
5 tablespoons margarine, melted
3 tablespoons hot milk
1 teaspoon vanilla extract
sugar-coated chocolate drops

1 Preheat the oven 350F. Grease two 8 inch cake pans, line each base with waxed paper, then grease the paper.

2 Sift the flour, baking powder, cocoa and salt into a large bowl. Stir in the sugar, then make a well in the center. Beat the eggs with the milk, vanilla and 5 tablespoons of water, then add to the dry ingredients with the margarine and beat until blended.

3 Divide the mixture equally between the 2 prepared pans. Burst any large air bubbles with the point of a knife, then bake the cakes for 20–25 minutes, or until springy to the touch.

4 Cool the layers for a few minutes, then turn out of the pans and peel off the lining papers. Leave the layers, the right way up, on a wire rack to cool.

5 Make the filling and topping: Sift the confectioner's sugar and cocoa powder into a bowl, then beat in the margarine, milk and vanilla. Leave for 15–30 minutes, to begin to thicken.

6 Place 1 layer on a serving plate and spread with half the chocolate mixture. Place the other layer on top and spread the top and sides with the remaining chocolate mixture. Decorate with sugar-coated drops. Leave for about 30 minutes, to firm, before cutting.

7 The finished cake will keep for about 4 days in an airtight container.

CHOCOLATE BANANA POPS

Freezing time: 6 hours
Preparation time: 15 minutes
Serves 4

2 bananas
4 oz semi-sweet chocolate, broken into pieces
1 tablespoon margarine or butter
1 tablespoon milk
½ cup shelled walnuts, chopped (optional)

1 Cut the bananas across into 4 equal pieces, then push a toothpick into the side of each piece of banana. Wrap the banana pieces in aluminium foil and freeze for about 6 hours or until firm.

2 Put the chocolate and margarine or butter into a bowl and place over a pan of gently simmering water until melted. Gradually stir in the milk, then remove the pan from the heat, but leave the bowl positioned over the hot water.

3 Remove the banana pieces from the freezer. Holding each banana piece by its stick, dip it into the chocolate mixture and turn it quickly to coat it on all sides.

4 If using walnuts, put the chopped nuts in a bowl and dip each chocolate-covered banana pop into the bowl to coat it evenly. Stick the toothpicks into half a grapefruit and leave to set. Once the chocolate is set and the banana thawed, the pops are ready to eat.

SPACESHIP CAKE

Preparation time: 1 hour
Baking time: 1–1¼ hours
Cooling time: 24 hours
Assembly time: 1½–2 hours
Serves 6–8

butter and flour for pans
chocolate and vanilla cake mixture (see page 39)
1 cup chocolate butter cream (see page 13)
bare 1 cup confectioner's sugar
8 mint-flavored chocolate sticks
4 chocolate discs, about 1 inch across
1 ice cream cone
½ cup green frosting (see page 90)
1 package sugar wafers
sugar-coated chocolate drops
spearmint gumdrops, quartered
1 mint-chocolate wafer
1 model spaceman (optional)

1 Preheat the oven to 325F. Butter and flour a 14 oz empty can and two 3½ cup ovenproof bowls. Quarter-fill the can with chocolate cake batter and half-fill one bowl with chocolate and one with vanilla cake batter. Bake the can for 30–35 minutes and the bowls for 1–1¼ hours. Cool for 10 minutes, then turn on to a wire rack and leave for 24 hours.

2 Sandwich the bowl cakes with chocolate butter cream, to make a globe. Cut the rounded end off the cylindrical cake and stick it on with frosting for a base.

3 Cover with chocolate butter cream and invert onto a board. Surround the base with unsifted confectioner's sugar "snow". Prop the spaceship with 2 mint-chocolate sticks at each quarter point, resting the bases on the chocolate discs.

4 Cut out the middle section of the ice cream cone and stand it inside the base of the cone. Put the pointed end on top and attach with green frosting.

5 Cut 6 "fins" from the sugar wafers. Make cuts in the cone with a sharp knife and insert the fins (see picture).

6 Cut strips of wafer and position to form two ledges (see picture). Cut more fins to place vertically at the intersections. Pipe green frosting on the edges of the wafers. Arrange colored, sugar-coated chocolate drops and quartered spearmint gumdrops to simulate lights. Position the chocolate wafer to form a ramp. Stand the model spaceman (if using) next to it.

CASTLE CAKE

Preparation time: 2 hours
Cooling time: 8 hours
Assembly time: 1 hour
Serves 12–14

- chocolate cake mixture (see page 84), divided, and baked in 2 deep, 6½ inch square pans
- 6 tablespoons red jam
- ¾ cup chocolate hazelnut spread
- 8 chocolate-covered mini-rolls
- 2 packets of lime jello
- 3 chocolate-covered wafers
- diamond gumdrop cake decorations
- colored dragees
- 3 × 2 oz triangular chocolate bars
- toy knights (optional)

1 Trim the cakes, if necessary, and sandwich with the jam. Trim off the corners and place the cake on a board.

2 Cover the cakes with chocolate hazelnut spread. Press 1 mini-roll against each corner, trim the top level and stick the remaining rolls on top with chocolate spread, to make turrets.

3 Make up the lime jello, pour into shallow trays and leave to set in the refrigerator.

4 Coat the undersides of the chocolate wafers with chocolate spread and arrange them on the board for a drawbridge. Use the chocolate spread to stick them down. Use diamond gumdrops and dragees to make the portcullis on the front of the cake.

5 Make the battlements by trimming the triangular chocolate bars to fit between the turrets; use the trimmings for the back edge.

6 Make windows with diamond gumdrops and stick a ring of dragees on top of each turret with chocolate spread, for battlements.

7 Just before serving, break up the jello and arrange around the cake to represent the moat. Place the toy knights in position, if using.

CHOCOLATE DOUGHNUT RINGS

Preparation time: 35 minutes
Cooling time: 40 minutes
Finishing time: 20 minutes
Makes 12

2¼ cups all-purpose flour
pinch of salt
½ teaspoon baking powder
4 tablespoons butter, melted
2 eggs, beaten
4 tablespoons granulated sugar
½ cup plus 2 tablespoons milk
oil, for deep-frying
granulated sugar, for coating
6 oz semi-sweet chocolate

1. Sift the flour, salt and baking powder together and make a well in the center.

2. Combine the butter, half the egg and the caster sugar and pour into the flour mixture. Stir well.

3. Heat the milk until warm and add to the butter and flour mixture. Stir until the flour is absorbed.

4. Cut the dough into 12 pieces and roll 12 sausages about 4 inches long. Form each sausage into a ring, sticking the ends together with the remaining beaten egg.

5. Heat the oil in a deep-frier or heavy sauce pan to 350F. Fry 4 rings and drain on paper towels. Dip one side of each doughnut in sugar while still hot. Repeat for the remaining 2 batches. Melt the chocolate (see page 9) and dip the unsugared side of each doughnut into the molten chocolate, to coat. Then allow to set.

CHOCOLATE WALNUT FUDGE

Preparation time: 15 minutes
Chilling time: 3–4 hours
Makes about 36 squares

- 9 oz chocolate sponge cake (stale cake works well in this recipe)
- ½ cup light soft brown sugar, firmly packed
- 1 stick or ½ cup margarine or butter
- 4 tablespoons light corn syrup
- 2 tablespoons cocoa powder
- ½ cup walnut pieces, coarsely chopped

1 Line a 6 inch square cake pan with foil, smoothing it well over the base and sides of the pan and well into the corners. Break the cake up into fine crumbs.

2 Put the sugar, margarine or butter and syrup into a saucepan and heat gently, stirring constantly, until the fat has melted and the sugar dissolved. Remove the pan from the heat, and stir in the cake crumbs, cocoa and nuts.

3 Turn the mixture into the prepared pan and smooth the surface with a palette knife. Leave to cool for about 30 minutes, then refrigerate for 3–4 hours, or until the fudge is firm.

4 To serve: cut the walnut fudge into 1 inch cubes, then place each cake in paper cases on a serving plate.

VARIATIONS
Replace the walnuts with almonds, pecans or broken Brazil nuts, or use seedless raisins or golden raisins.

CAT'S EYES CAKES

Preparation time: 50 minutes
Cooling time: 30 minutes
Makes 16–18 cakes

1 cup plus 2 tablespoons all-purpose flour
2 tablespoons cocoa powder
½ teaspoon baking powder
½ cup granulated sugar
1 stick or 1 cup butter, softened
2 eggs
½ teaspoon vanilla extract
¾ cup chocolate chips
about 2 tablespoons milk

FROSTING
3 oz semi-sweet chocolate
3 tablespoons butter
pinch of salt
1⅔ cups confectioner's sugar, sifted
2–3 drops green food coloring

1. Preheat the oven to 375F.

2. In a mixing bowl, sift together the flour, cocoa and baking powder. In another bowl, beat the sugar and butter together until the mixture is light and fluffy, then gradually beat in the eggs. Add the vanilla, then stir in the sifted ingredients a little at a time.

3. Stir in the chocolate chips and beat in enough milk to give the mixture a soft, dropping consistency.

4. Put 16–18 paper cupcake cases on a baking sheet and half-fill them with the mixture. Bake the cakes for 20 minutes or until they are well risen and firm. Remove from the oven, place on a wire rack and leave to cool.

5. Make the chocolate frosting: Melt the chocolate and butter in a bowl over simmering water.

6. Remove from the heat and beat well. Beat in 3 tablespoons hot water and a pinch of salt. Gradually add ¾ cup of confectioner's sugar and beat until smooth. Leave to cool, then spread the frosting over the cakes and leave it to set.

7. Decorate the cakes: Mix the remaining ½ cup confectioner's sugar with enough cold water to make a piping consistency. Using a waxed paper piping bag fitted with a small plain nozzle, pipe eyebrows and long whiskers on each face.

8. Color the remaining frosting green with food coloring and pipe on the eyes.

CHOCOLATE FONDUE

Preparation time: 30 minutes
Cooking time: 10 minutes
Serves 12

14 oz semi-sweet chocolate, broken into pieces
1¼ cups heavy cream
6 tablespoons orange juice
4 tablespoons unsalted butter

DIPPERS
8 inch sponge cake
apricot jam, for spreading
4 large bananas
2 tablespoons lemon juice
2 large eating apples
16 oz can sliced peaches in syrup, well drained
other fruits, if liked

1 First prepare the dippers: Slice the cake in half horizontally and sandwich with apricot jam. Cut into neat 1 inch cubes. Peel the bananas, cut into slices ½ inch thick and toss in 1 tablespoon lemon juice. Quarter, core and slice the apples and toss in the remaining lemon juice. Leave peach slices whole, or cut into chunks if large. Prepare all the fresh fruit as soon as possible before serving to prevent them from discoloring.

2 Make the fondue: Put the chocolate into a heavy-based fondue pan or small saucepan and add the cream and orange juice.

3 Just before serving, gently heat the chocolate, cream and orange juice together until the chocolate melts, stirring all the time. Continue until almost, but not quite boiling. Do not let the chocolate mixture boil or it will separate. Stir in the butter until melted.

4 Place the pan over a small alcohol burner on the table. Arrange the cake and fruit around the fondue, along with fondue or ordinary forks.

VARIATIONS
Use 1 lb pound cake in place of sponge. Use other well drained, canned or fresh fruits.

INDEX